Historical Sketches Of Roswell Franklin & Family, Drawn Up At The Request Of Stephen Franklin

Robert Hubbard

Alpha Editions

This Edition Published in 2021

ISBN: 9789354506970

Design and Setting By
Alpha Editions
www.alphaedis.com
Email – info@alphaedis.com

As per information held with us this book is in Public Domain.
This book is a reproduction of an important historical work. Alpha Editions uses the best technology to reproduce historical work in the same manner it was first published to preserve its original nature. Any marks or number seen are left intentionally to preserve its true form.

HISTORICAL SKETCHES

OF

ROSWELL FRANKLIN

AND FAMILY.

DRAWN UP AT THE REQUEST OF
STEPHEN FRANKLIN,

BY ROBERT HUBBARD.

DANSVILLE, N. Y.
PRINTED BY A. STEVENS.
1839.

HISTORICAL SKETCHES, &c.

CHAPTER I.

Mr. Franklin enlists as a soldier in the British army—Goes to Canada—Thence to the West Indies—Returns to Connecticut—Marries—Goes to Wyoming—Is put into jail at Easton—Breaks jail and escapes—Brings on his family to Wyoming—Is engaged in several skirmishes with the Pennamites, and with the Indians.

This narrative has the advantage of being literally true, bating a few inaccuracies inseparable from such a work. It was taken down from the mouths of the surviving members of the family, to wit, Olive Stevens and Roswell and Stephen Franklin; all of whom are now living and in full possession of their faculties. Those parts of the story which relate to their father, they often heard him recount when they were young, and lived at home; which, together with the other scenes in which they were personally concerned, made too deep an impression upon their young and tender minds ever to be forgotten. I mention these circumstances, not because there is any thing marvellous or improbable in any part of the narrative, but because people generally, when they read a book, like to know whether it be fact or only fiction.

The scene of much of the story is the beautiful and celebrated valley of Wyoming, a wide level on both sides of the Susquehannah, in the state of Pennsylvania, bounded by hills, in some places lofty and precipitous, in others, of more gentle ascent; but on the whole, a most desiraole situation, where, on the rich alluvial flats, the poor Indian might cultivate his corn, and on the hills might hunt the deer and the bear. The river, also, before the encroachment of the whites, afforded him abundance of fish, and a fine road for his canoe. The cupidity and superior skill and enterprize of the pale man, wrested or won this fertile possession from his red brother. It became the scene of contention and bloodshed. The Indians were in part avenged by the wars which their spoilers had among themselves. They invaded and disturbed one another, and shed each others blood; and in this way God chastised them for their injustice to the original owners of the soil. White men warred with white men, and not with Indians alone.

It might, at first view, be supposed that the writer was the advocate of war. But it is not so. He believes that the spirit of war is not the spirit of Christ, and of course, that war itself is anti-christian. There ought to be no such thing as war, and would not be if men were thoroughly disposed to do right. There may be cases in which self-defence is justifiable, is even an imperative duty; but there are many modes of self defence which may be practised without a resort to the shedding of human blood. If the blood of man must be shed at all, it ought to be felt to be a solemn and awful thing to shed it. It ought to be done as a point of obedience to God, and of purely benevolent love to man. This is duty in every thing.— We are required to do all we do in love, and even to love our enemies. This is not the spirit of war. If I kill my fellow man, be he ever so bitter an enemy, it ought to be done with as pure an intention as would be required in any other act. The laws of God, and the example of Christ, require it.— Thou shalt love thy neighbor as thyself, is a precept which the Supreme lawgiver never alters. It is binding upon all men, at all times. Some have attempted to plead the example of the Israelites to justify war. But this is not to the point. They were employed, under a special commission from God, to execute criminals who had forfeited their lives to his justice. He made known his will to them in the matter by an explicit revelation. When nations or individuals, at this day, can shew the same authority, under the broad seal of heaven, which the Israelites had, they may be authorized to do as they did, and not till then.

This narrative (with the addition of a few years before and after) belongs to the era of the revolution, that well known period so rich in characters and events of high bearing and thrilling interest. I wish I were able to give some detail of the events belonging to the early youth of the hero of my story, as it would probably unfold several speci-

1*

mens of that quick nerve & adventurous spirit which he displayed in subsequent life. All I know is that he became a soldier a few years previous to the war of the revolution, when this country and England were one. First he went with a body of troops to the borders of Canada, and afterwards joined the British army, and went with it, as a private soldier, to the West Indies. On the passage out, he with others, was cast away upon a desolate Island, where they suffered intolerably from heat and thirst; the casks of fresh water being stove, and their provision, the little they saved, made salt and unpalatable by having been wetted with sea water. The suffering of men in such a climate, and under such a sun, when destitute of fresh water, are dreadful beyond description. The fever of the throat and stomach burns intensely, produces the most raging thirst, and mocks all relief, except that which may be afforded by a supply of fresh water. It is a most distressing case, which can be fully known only by those who have felt it. In such a situation the most violent stickler for alcohol would speedily become a cold water man

Two other vessels were shipwrecked at the same time by the ignorance or carelessness of the pilots. Probably rum was at the bottom of the whole of it, it being a probable calculation that about three-fourths of the shipwrecks which have happened in former years might have been avoided but for the use of intoxicating drinks, either by the captain or crew, or both. They all had to stay fourteen days with nothing to defend them from the scorching rays of a West Indian sun, and with no other relief but a single shower, to catch which they spread out every piece of linen, or clothing, and every rag they could muster. These, when wet, they wrung out into a dish, or eagerly put to their lips and sucked out the delicious juice, more pleasant to their taste than the finest lemonade would have been at a common time. The other vessels had to go to Havannah, the capital of the island of Cuba, and return. After fourteen days suffering they were taken off, and sailed to join the fleet which lay in the harbor of the above named city. He was present and shared in the danger and fatigues of the siege of Havannah, where such numbers were killed, and so many swept away by pestilence. Not a few of the hardy sons of New England found their graves here. Many were swept away by the terrible fever of the climate; but the subject of this narrative was spared, God having designed him, as we shall see, for other events, and further services. It is probable that his West Indian campaign was a school, in which his active and courageous spirit was trained up for the hardships, difficulties and dangers which he was afterwards called to encounter. To say the least, he must have learnt something of men and things which he did not know before, and must have gained some experience in the stratagems, perils and fluctuations of war. The siege of Havannah was in the year 1762, and lasted two months and eight days. Mr. Franklin used to reckon the time twelve weeks, including (I suppose) all the time from the first approach of the fleet to its final departure from the harbor. The siege was carried on with great animosity of feeling, and energy of action. The English were stirred up to the utmost rage and fury of resentment by the cruelties of the Spaniards, who took some of the prisoners which had fallen into their hands and hung them up alive in chains, upon trees, outside of the walls of the city, where they were seen by the besiegers, and where they were left to die by inches in intolerable agony, and to be devoured by birds of prey.

This provoked retaliation, to what extent I do not know, only that Mr. Franklin used to relate that they put dead bodies into their mortars, with their bombs, and threw their scattered fragments, in showers of corruption, over the walls into the city, and tainted the air and filled the minds of the citizens with dismal forebodings of what must befal them if the city were taken by storm. These apprehensions of the inhabitants probably hastened the signing of articles of capitulation, for Mr. Franklin, when he afterwards saw the means of defence which they possessed within the city, supposed that they might have stood it out some time longer, if they had not been moved by fear.

Soon after the city surrendered Mr. Franklin returned to his native place, Woodbury, Litchfield county, Connecticut. Here he married and settled down, having left the army. Probably his term of service had expired. He remained here about eight years before he removed to the Susquehannah.— Not very far from this time a company of men belonging to Connecticut, purchased land of the Indians, to whom belonged the valley of Wyoming, and paid them for it in silver money. The company, I suppose, thought they had a right to purchase this land of the aborigines, notwithstanding it lay within the State of Pennsylvania, from the fact that the original charter, granted by Charles I, king of England, to the early settlers of Connecticut, allowed it a certain width, north and south, and then to to run back, between these lines, due west, till it reached the western ocean. This, if my memory serves me, was the grant. The valley of Wyoming was judged to be within these lines, and belonged, therefore, to Connecticut. Hers was the older title, but was not admitted to be valid by Pennsylvania. This opposition of claims between the two states occasioned quarrels between the people. Mr. Franklin, however, and many others, took farms under this title, believing it to be good, and in the year 1770 moved on his family. It was concerning this very spot of land that the contest arose between the Pennsylvanians and Yankees, known by the name of the Pennamite war, a short time before the war of the revolution. It began with fists, proceeded to clubs, and finally ended with guns. The Pennamites began and attacked the Yankees and drove them off the ground, but held it not long, for the other party soon came upon them and made them flee in their turn. The Connecticut people, after this, built a fort. Not long after an attempt was made to take it, by one Ogden. As he approached, he was warned by the commanding officer of the fort, not to pass a certain line, if he did he was a dead man. Ogden, in return, swore he would eat his breakfast that morning in the fort, or in hell. The officer had a little fellow under his command named Donald, or Daniels, a keen shot, to whom he said, "Daniels, when I give the word, do you put a ball through that man." He gave the word and the fatal bullet pierced him through, and he fell dead in his tracks, and all his party took to their heels and ran away. So sudden and fearful was the end of the fool hardy blasphemer! One moment he was swaggering and swearing here in the body—the next moment his guilty soul, unwashed and unpardoned, passes into the unseen world, and falls into the hands of the living God, to be judged according to his works.

This fatal gun was the first which was fired by the Yankee party. It was followed by a succession of quarrels, disturbances and bloodshed.

One event belonging to the personal history of Mr. Franklin, must have occurred about the time when he brought on his family, or rather a few months previous; that is, in the spring of the year 1770.

He was involved, as a matter of course, in the Pennamite war, and was taken prisoner and put into Easton jail. The circumstances of the affair, as I have understood them, were these. He, and others with him, were on their way to Connecticut to bring their families. One night they took lodgings at a house on the Jersey side of the Delaware, opposite Easton. The Pennamites came upon them in the night, laid hands on them and put them into prison. Their friends heard of their capture and talked of attempting a rescue. This came to the ears of the Pennamites, and they changed their treatment of the prisoners. They had supplied them, at first, with a sufficient variety and plenty of provisions, but now they compelled them to live upon bread and water. They also brought fire-arms and ammunition into the jail, not fewer than twenty-five muskets, and engaged men to stand in readiness to aid the jailer, if their help should be wanted. This lean fare did not suit the prisoners, who, having been accustomed to stronger food, were not disposed to sit down contented with such provision. They thought about it, and talked it over among themselves. This is harder, said Franklin, than I fare at home, and I won't stay. The others felt as he did, and determined to regain their liberty, and set themselves about forming their plans for it immediately. It was an undertaking attended with considerable difficulty and some danger. They were kept up stairs and well secured with locks and bolts.— Twice a day, however, they were let down for refreshment, and admitted into a back yard where was a well. Great caution was employed. Only four were permitted to go down at a time, and they must return before any more were suffered to descend. This was all the liberty they had, and afforded the only chance of escape. In addition to this, they would be under the necessity of operating in broad day light, and of forcing their way through the midst of their enemies at the hazard of losing their lives in the attempt. The perils of the enterprize are apparent upon the face of it. Nothing effective could be done without a well devised plan and a vigorous execution. They must have a leader; and who should he be? It was agreed, among themselves, that the next four who should go down; of whom Franklin would be one, should be leaders in the business. To effect their enlargement it was necessary that they should get out at the front door into the street; but how to get the key was the pinch. To forward their design one of the prisoners pretended to be sick, and was taken below to receive medical aid. His object was to find out where they deposited the big key, and he kept an eye out upon their movements, but watched in vain. He discovered, indeed, that it was kept in different places at different times, but could not ascertain any one spot as the place of deposit where they would be always sure to find it. The man soon got better and was taken up again. They then consulted together and fixed on a time to commence their attempt. It was to be in the afternoon, and on such a day, near at hand. It was finally decided that Franklin should be captain. Well, said he, I am the smallest among you, but will undertake upon this proviso: If we should fail of regaining our liberty you shall not fling all the blame upon me, but shall bear your share of it. To this they all assented.

It may be well here to bear in mind that fire-arms, and powder and ball had been brought into the jail since their confinement to guard it against an apprehended attack from the Yankees. And it may be remarked also, that the jailor, having occasion to go away that afternoon, let them down two or three hours earlier than usual, which favored their plan, as it gave them more time for its execution. One other favorable circumstance may be noticed. Two or three men, who lived near, came in that afternoon to help the jailor, if he should need, and with them a blacksmith, who brought his hammer, and laid it on one of the jail windows.— We shall see the use which was made of this hammer thus opportunely, without their seeking, provided for them. These men went into the yard with the jailor, and his wife came, with her knitting, and sat in the door. Franklin had previously directed his three companions to be on the lookout, near the door, and not to scatter. He then steps up to the jailor, who was a good humored man, and puts his hand familiarly upon his shoulder, and says, though I have been shut up here so close, and fed on such weak stuff as bread and water, I'll bet a trifle, after all, that I can beat you at hopping. He then made a mark near the door, and hopped off as far as he could at three hops. The jailor next comes up to it. Stop, says the other, till I come back and see that you start fair. As soon as the jailor began his hop, Franklin jumps to the door, gives it a violent swing, sweeps the woman, with her knitting, into the yard, and immediately turns the key, which was in the door, and locks up her and her husband, and the two or three attendants, closely enough. The next thing was to liberate the prisoners above. He espied the blacksmith's hammer in the window, where it had been carelessly left by its owner. It was the very thing he wanted. He seized it and went to work with all his might. While he was engaged in breaking the locks, the jailer and his company in the back yard were crying murder, as loud as they could bawl, and the people of the town were alarmed, and were rallying and hastening to their aid as fast as possible. Having succeeded in letting the prisoners out of the rooms in the upper part of the jail, they had still to hunt for the key of the front door, which opened into the street. It was found at last among some papers, in the drawer of a mahogany table, which they broke open, scattering the papers about the floor. While things were a going on at this rate within the jail, the whole body of the villagers were collected about the front door, and in the street, with the full purpose of arresting the prisoners should they venture abroad, and with the expectation, no doubt, that they could terrify them by their numbers into immediate submission, and prevent them from making further efforts to escape. But the citizens, in the hurry and confusion of the moment, had brought no arms with them, and probably did not, just then, recollect how well they had supplied the unruly Yankees with them. They had provided guns, powder and ball for the purpose of keeping them safely; and now, behold, these are the very things by which these mischievous fellows are able to clear their way in spite of the overwhelming numbers of their enemies. The party within were now prepared to sally forth, with their loaded muskets in their hands, and their brave and cautious leader at their head. They did so; and the authority called upon the citizens to seize them. Their captain told his men to keep together in a solid column, and they would pass safely. As they marched out a man stepped up to Franklin to seize him. It was a critical moment; the least hesitation might have ruined the enterprize. Our hero's presence of mind did not fail him. He said to his assailant, sir, it is a case of life and death, and if you presume to lay hands on me you are a dead man. The man drew back, and the crowd which had gathered opened a lane and suffered them to pass right through the midst, not daring to touch such resolute men, whom they saw so well prepared to defend themselves. Not a hand was raised; not a tongue muttered; a dead silence reigned on every side, and the little band of heroes marched through in safety. They saw it was death to touch them. Thus far courage and conduct were united. But there is a difference between real courage, joined with sound discretion, which can stand and act alone, and that conventional bravery which depends upon numbers and circumstances. This difference was soon apparent in the conduct of the men who had just escaped from prison. They had passed beyond the bounds of the village, away from the immediate view of their enemies, and considered themselves

out of danger. Their leader did not think so.—
Though more resolute in action than any of them,
he was not fool-hardy; he did not lose his judgement
by a little present success. He was convinced
that their entire deliverance required that they
should continue to march in a body, keeping their
guns loaded, and maintaining a good lookout So
he told them But they felt too foolishly confident
and joyful to regard his advice. "Oh," they said,
"there was no fear ; they could take care of themselves;
they would run the risk of being taken
again." When he saw their folly, and perceived
that they had no mind to regard the promise they
had made to him of keeping together, judging that
further effort on his part would avail nothing, he
ceased to expostulate with them, and quietly permitted
them to take their own course. Being much
fatigued, he gave up his gun to one of them, and
bade them shirk for themselves, and left them to
go their own way, while he went his, by himself
alone. As he conjectured, so it actually happened;
they scattered and were every one of them retaken
and put back into their old place of confinement,
not long after. Thus it is that advantages
are lost, and disasters brought on, by self confidence
and the neglect to follow good advice. We
may pity the poor fellows picked up, here and there,
one by one, but we need not wonder at it, nor think
it strange, if they felt dispirited and ashamed to
find themselves so soon in their old cage again.

As for our hero, having given up his gun, he
went up to a bush pasture not far distant, where he

found a place of concealment and hid himself and lay and rested till dark. At dark he arose and cut a good sized hickory stick, which might answer either for a staff to walk with, or for a club to fight with, if he should need one for his own defence. Thus equipped, and possessing both caution and courage, in no common degree, he laid his course directly for Easton. Having arrived at the village, he walked down the main street, through the town, to the Delaware river. He saw dimly, through the dusky light of the evening, several persons along the road but he kept himself aloof from them, and no one discovered who he was, nor in the least suspected that it was one of the prisoners who had so lately broken away from their jail.— At the river he found a canoe, and paddled across into the state of New Jersey, and then set his little vessel adrift, and away it floated down the river. Darkness, silence and loneliness reigned around him. He heard nothing save the low, sullen murmurs of the waters, and saw neither friend nor foe to cheer his sadness or stir his fears. A solitary wanderer amid the darkness of the night—what shall he do? Whither shall he go? To stay where he is will be detection and death, or at best, imprisonment; for the light of the morrow's sun will expose him to the view of his enemies. From them he can expect nothing but the most rigorous confinement, and the hardest usage for having so completely outwited them. If he would travel abroad into the country, he knows not where to go, nor into whose hands he may fall. He has not a coat to

2*

his back, is wet and hungry, and begins to feel the effects of a severe cold caught and settled deeply upon him, by great fatigues and unseasonable exposures. But cold or hungry, wet or dry, sick or well, he has a family dear to his affections, many miles off, and he feels that he must press forward through every hindrance, to meet them This moved him to effort, and would not permit him to sink into despondency. So he wandered on, not knowing whither he went, amid the darkness of the night. In the morning he found that he was still in the vicinity of Easton, for he could hear the drums beat to call the people to arms; probably to follow and retake him and the others who had broken jail with him. Nearly exhausted, he said to himself, I may as well die one way as another; I will venture to call at this house before me; it may be that I shall find friends, and if not, I may as well fall into the hands of my enemies and be killed as to starve myself to death. Full of concern upon the subject, feeling that he put his life into his hand, yet driven by hunger and distress, he ventured to go in. He accosted the man of the house, entered into conversation with him, endeavored to draw out his sentiments, and found him apparently friendly to the Connecticut people. To this man he frankly related the story of his breaking jail, laid open to him his true situation, and did not attempt to conceal his wants or his intentions. In conclusion, he said to him, you see how the case is with me, if you deceive me you may as well take my life at once, I am in your hands, and have no power to fight or run at present. The man assured him he need not fear, he would not betray him to his enemies, but would defend him at the hazard of his life. Having cheered him by his words, he next ordered victuals for his refreshment, and when he had done eating, furnished him with a bed where he might rest his weary bones and muscles. Here he lay down and fell asleep, not knowing what might befall him. But whether his enemies came upon him or not, he could live no longer without sleep. Every member of his body, and every faculty of his mind cried out for it. He lay for some hours buried in profound slumbers, and then awoke, recruited in strength and revived in spirits, and girded up his loins for the long walk which he had yet to take. His good natured host gave him instructions what course to pursue to find his family, who were living comfortably, as he hoped, in Woodbury, in good old Connecticut. Having thanked him for his kindness, and for his unbought faithfulness, he set forward and arrived safely at his own quiet and happy home.

This was in the spring, or early in the summer. He passed the season in Woodbury, and in autumn started with his family for Pennsylvania It was late before they reached the place of their destination. They had cold rains to encounter, and the ground was frozen before they finished their journey. This last circumstance was an advantage, for they had a wilderness and a great swamp to cross, east of the valley of the Susquehannah, rearly or quite impassable with a team except when frozen over. Without any adverse occurrence they found themselves quietly seated, at length, on the fertile banks of the beautiful Susquehannah. They rested not long. War was on their borders, and Mr. Franklin was very active in defending the settlement in which his family lived, against an attack from a party of Pennsylvanians. This was before the war of the revolution, in what year is not distinctly remembered, but supposed to be in the year 1793. An invasion was set on foot, headed by a Col. Plunket, and afterwards known by the name of Plunket's expedition.

Plunket, and 4 0 men under his command, came up the river in boats. The object was to drive off the Yankees, plunder their settlements and return down the river with the spoils. The Yankees could muster about as many to oppose them; and these were men of nerve and vigor. They fought for their wives and children, and their homes, and all the interests which cluster around them. And, so far as can be judged at this distance of time, appear to have had justice on their side.— They fought in self defence against those who came uncommanded by public authority. to drive them from their possessions. Plunket and his party had several boats, two of which contained provisions, and ammunition. The time was just before Christmas. The attack was made, and skirmishing was had, at first, near the Shawney flats, below Wilksbarre, on the west side of the Susquenannah. The Yankees, in the first place, built and fortified a camp, in which they

thought of making a stand against the enemy.—
But when they came to examine the situation, and
saw that it was surrounded by higher lands, which
completely overlooked it, they concluded to abandon it. They retired farther back to higher
ground, and chose a side hill in the woods, in a very advantageous position for defence, where they
built a stout breastwork of logs, and determined
to make a stand against their invaders. Plunket,
lifted up with a high conceit of his military prowess and puissant force, told his men that the Yankees dared not fight him, and boastingly swore that
he would take his Christmas supper in the fort.—
His expectation was, that he should drive the Yankees from one position to another, or rather that
they would flee before him till they finally huddled
into the fort, and that then he should terrify or
compel them into an immediate surrender, with little or no fighting. With this fond idea of self-complacent pride in his head, he left the river with
the main body of his men, and pushed forward across the flat after the Yankees till he came to their
deserted camp. When he saw it he crowed mightily. There, said he, look there, I told you they
would not dare to fight. The men caught the spirit of their leader, and onward they pressed in hot
persuit of the flying foe. Thus they continued till
they came to the foot of the hill and began to climb
its side, through the woods. They slowly ascended and kept on their way till they drew near the
fortified spot, which they did not discover till within a short distance of it. It seems to have struck

their sight quite unexpectedly, and Plunket bawled
out, there is breastwork. The words were scarcely out of his mouth before a shower of balls whistled about his ears. The fire was returned by Plunket's men, and the fight continued for some
time, but the assailants could get no further. They
found they had to do with men who knew what
they were about and who made their enemies know
it too. Mr. Franklin, who acted as lieutenant under a colonel whose name is not remembered, kept
a very careful and critical lookout upon the enemy,
being jealous that though they should be defeated
here, they might do mischief elsewhere. He kept
a particular watch of the boats, which lay in sight,
fearing for the defenceless women and children left
in the settlements, especially in the largest one,
which was situated on the eastern side of the river
at no great distance below them. While he was
thus on the lookout, he saw the enemy clear out a
boat and cross the river and bring over a man, and
soon after cross again. He saw also other boats,
manned with armed men, preparing to go somewhere, and he was finally convinced either they
intended to make a final retreat, or more probably,
to go over and fall upon the settlement, and pillage,
and perhaps burn it in the absence of the men. He
therefore made immediate application to his colonel,
who objected first to his going, but afterwards gave
him liberty to pick his men, as many as he wanted,
and pass over to the other side and be ready to meet
the plunderers, and give them a warm reception
should they attempt to land. But they had many

things to detain them. In the first place they could not find a boat, canoe, or any thing of the kind near, and had to go up the river some distance to procure one. Then the one which they found was nothing but a canoe, and that a poor leaky thing. In addition to this, the crossing was attended with hazard on account of the anchor ice which floated in the river, and dashed against the sides of the canoe. And one thing more, they had but little time in which they could act, it being late in the afternoon. With all these difficulties in the way, it was only barely possible for them to get over and reach the landing place below soon enough to prevent the enemy from falling upon their wives and children. Their souls, however, were up, and they made every nerve and muscle work hard, determined to gain their point or perish in the attempt. The effort was noble, but a dark uncertainty hovered over the issue of it, nor could they be relieved from anxiety till they reached the point at which they aimed. It was after sunset when they had all got over. Not a moment was to be lost, it might be too late even then; they passed rapidly down the eastern bank of the river, three miles, to the place where they expected the enemy to land. Every man had his gun loaded and his hand on the lock ready to fire. They arrived just at the instant when their foes were about to land. It was dark, but they heard the boats grind upon the anchor ice, close to the shore, the moment after they arrived, Franklin discharged his musket at the enemy, and then jumped right down the bank between the two parties, allowing them to fire over his head. His men instantly poured in their shot as thick as hail, and made all ring again. The boats were so near that Mr. Franklin said he could have thrown his gun into them. It was close and warm work, and must have been bloody but for the darkness which enveloped them, and the hurry in which they fired. The poor fellows on board had no notice of an enemy, and expected no resistance till they saw the blaze and heard the roar of the musketry just about their heads. They made no attempt to land, but returned the fire, and after they had discharged their pieces, lay flat in the bottom of their boats and let the bullets fly over them. In the mean time they suffered the boats to be carried down the river by the force of the current till they got beyond the reach of the shot. The party on shore, however, followed them, and intended to continue the pursuit, till they drove them over the rapids, but were stopped by a creek, the ice of which was not strong enough to bear them. By means of this the boats were saved from destruction. It gave them opportunity to land above the falls and wait for daylight, instead of being hurried over in the night, when they could not see how to steer, nor where to go. Thus, by the good providence of God, the lives of both the contending bodies were spared; the one having to flee from the ground, the other being stopped in the pursuit.

This rapid and well timed movement of our hero, and the brave men who were with him, under God, saved the settlement from immediate ruin without the loss of a man. How many of the invaders fell is not known.

How much one such man was worth to that settlement at that time, and how dear he, and his faithful associates, must have been to the tender hearted mothers who, together with their children, were saved from plunder, and from alarms still more distressing, we need not attempt to describe. But for his watchful promptness and extreme activity, they must have fallen into the hands of the enemy. It affords an important lesson on the subject of doing things promptly, and at the right time. Much is gained by it. On the other hand, much is lost by indecision, by delays, by lingering. A weak character loses almost every advantage put into his hands, accomplishes nothing to what he might, and not unfrequently meets with ill success in those very situations where a resolute person goes ahead and prospers. Decision and punctuality are important points in the education of children. Let them be taught, when they have any thing on hand to do, to do it and not linger. Let this be seen to, and insisted on, without accepting any of their idle excuses.

Mr. Franklin's sagacity, activity and courage, seconded by his men, having beaten off the boats, seems to have been the cause of the immediate retreat of the whole party. They all cleared out the next day. Thus ended the vain boastings of Plunket and his host.

The Goodness of God is very visible in saving, so happily, the women and children from such an assault, and probably some among them might have felt a grateful sense of it.

This action was near the beginning of the war. During its progress, Mr. Franklin and family, living as they did in a frontier settlement, were much exposed, and frequently disturbed. At different times, both before and after the battle of Wyoming, in the year 1778, the settlers were disturbed by the incursions of the Indians. They would keep watch upon the hills, and when they thought the opportunity favorable, would rush down in the night, and sometimes in the day time, and come suddenly upon a house and plunder and burn it, and carry off the women and children, unless they chose to kill them, or a part of them. Sometimes they would waylay the road and attempt to shoot, or take prisoners, those who passed. It was distressing to live so. To go to bed with the thought that probably your house might be assaulted in the night, or else that the lurking foe might shoot you in the morning as soon as you should venture abroad, and rush into the house over your prostrate and wounded body, and sieze upon your defenceless family and hurry them off into captivity, could not be a comfortable thought. It might possibly be borne, and that would be all. Such was their situation, perilous, unsettled and full of discomfort. So it would be to us, in the extreme. They, however, bore it far better than we should, being accustomed to it, and being trained up in hardier habits.

Not far from this time, that is, in the early part

of the war, Mr. Franklin exchanged shots with the Indians several times, either alone or in company with others.

At one time, an old lady passing from one neighbor to another, reported that she had seen an Indian cross the path; but the fact was doubted, because she was subject to alarms not always well founded. The night following a gun was heard, which, it was supposed, was fired at wolves by some one of the settlers. Not far from the dawn of day, Mr. Franklin thought he heard a noise; he arose and opened, cautiously, his stout double doors, one of which swung in and the other out, and walked out of the house and cast his eye to a calf pasture. a few rods distant, and saw, dimly, two or three Indians. He stepped back in an instant, seized his loaded gun, and pointing it through a narrow opening of the doors, fired at them as they stood in one corner of the pasture, or as they passed slowly through it. Upon examination afterwards. blood was found on the fence, and the conclusion was that one or more of them must have been wounded.— They retreated and left him in quiet possession of his house. An alarm, however, was caused in the settlement, but no mischief was done. At another time he heard his hogs squeal, and concluded that the Indians were trying to carry them off and kill them. He determined to see what was the matter, and if they were stealing, to make them pay dearly for it. He stepped out with his gun, passed along behind a bush fence till he came opposite to where the Indians were, and stood watching, and when one of them rose up from butchering the hog, he drew up and shot him.

At another time he and others were upon a scouting expedition, and encountered a party of Indians in the woods. The white men had partly outflanked the Indians, which being perceived by the latter, they also extended their line and assumed, in some degree, the form of a half moon. Mr. Franklin stood at one end of the line, and saw an Indian at a distance, not directing his eyes toward the point where he stood, but apparently seeking to get a shot at somebody else in another quarter.— The Indian tried to shield himself behind a tree, and yet was so intent on killing his enemy that he exposed some part of his body, which Mr. Franklin perceiving, put a ball through him, and immediately ran up, seized his gun, stripped off his accoutrements, thought he would load both guns, and set one of them where he could find it, intending afterwards to scalp him; a thing he had never before done.

But while he was busy, another man seized the moment and took off the scalp.

Scalping is a barbarous custom learned of the Indians. An expert hand can perform it in an instant. A portion of hair, on the crown, is grasped with the left hand, a sharp knife in the right, cuts the skin in a circle, and then it is forcibly twitched off. This is sometimes done when the poor wounded wretch is yet alive, and while his groans continue to sound in the ears of his assailant. The action lasted a few minutes, perhaps fifteen or twenty, several shots were exchanged and the Indians fled. By a series of such exploits as these, being thorough in watching the motions of his enemies, and dextrous in cutting them up, taking every advantage of them, and giving them little chance to circumvent him, he had become well known to the Indians, and they hated and dreaded him, and greatly desired to get him into their power. Twice, at least, they came very near to it. Once in the battle of Wyoming, and once afterwards, when his family were taken prisoners.

CHAPTER II.

Battle of Wyoming—Confidence and appearance of victory on the part of the Americans—Sudden and fatal turn of the action against them—Efforts of Mr. Franklin to retrieve the disasters of the day—Narrowly escapes being killed—Returns to the fort and witnesses the grief of the women and children.

I proceed to give some account, as narrated by him, of the action between the Americans on the one side, and the British and Indians on the other, known by the name of the battle of Wyoming.—It was fought on the third of July, 1778. It was a fair and beautiful morning, and was followed by a hot day. It had been a matter of consultation and deliberation, beforehand, whether to go out and encounter their enemies in open fight, or remain within the fort and defend themselves there. They felt competent to either. The one course appeared more prudent, the other more brave. They chose the latter; partly because they were bold and enterprizing men, and partly because they hoped the sooner to rid themselves of their enemies. And further, in favor of advancing upon the foe, instead of waiting for him, it was apparent in case of defeat, they would still have the fort in their possession as a place of refuge for themselves, and especially as a means of defence for their families.

Having resolved upon a battle, they were not long in preparing for it, where almost every man was a soldier, and ready furnished with arms and ammunition. They marched out from the fort, in number between three and four hundred; or three hundred strong, as it is in the old ballad, which was written and published soon after the battle. The words are,

"Our men march'd out from the Forty Fort,
    The third day of July;
Three hundred strong, they march'd along,
    The fate of war to try."

The enemy were much more numerous. They have been rated as high as sixteen hundred, which is probably far too high an estimate. They might have been two to one, or perhaps more, which is a great disparity. Almost the whole company of Americans consisted of men drawn from the settlements in the valley of Wyoming A few were veteran soldiers, but the most of them were young men in their prime, of extraordinary vigor of muscle and nerve. A large proportion of these young men had wives in the settlement where they lived. Many of them, on the morning of the battle, saw their wives and children for the last time ; but they did not know it, nor had they time to indulge their feelings. They had other and rougher work to do. The women remained behind to weep. Many an affectionate wife on that fatal morning, followed with her heart and with her eyes, her dear, brave husband as he left her ; looked after him as long as she could see him ; and when she could see him no longer, sat down and wept. Many a fond and anxious mother thought of her son going out to be exposed to the bullets of a dreaded foe; thought of him, and trembled for him; wished and prayed that she might see him again; but oh! what if she should not—it was more than she could bear without tears and groans of anguish. There were daughters who felt deeply for their fathers, and sisters whose souls went out after their brothers. The lives of all who went out to the battle field that day, were inexpressibly dear to those who remained behind, for they were not strangers, or hired soldiers, but the fathers and husbands, sons and brothers of the afflicted women who stayed at home to watch, and think and mourn. By far the greater part of the men belonging to the valley were in the action. They strengthened their hearts and nerved their arms to defend their wives and children ; to drive back the invaders, and to provide for themselves a quiet home, where they might enjoy unmolested the fruits of their labours. All this they expected to obtain by gaining a decisive victory; and of this they were confident. Inspired by this strong anticipation of success, they began the fight with high spirits, and prosecuted it with vigor. And it appeared as if their expectations were about to be realized. The enemy began to fall back, and the battle seemed to be won. A few Indians were seen to make a stand behind a small swamp or swail, but the great body of them had fallen back and were out of sight. The ground was well fitted for an Indian fight, being of that description which is known by the name of oak openings, covered with large scattered oak trees and underbrush. These trees afforded a shelter to the combatants, from behind which they could watch their opportunity and shoot at their opponents without much exposure of their own persons. From tree to tree the enemy had retired and had been followed up, they evidently flagged and wavered, and the men of Wyoming seemed upon the point of a glorious victory, when suddenly a fatal turn was given to the events of the day, and every thing went against them. A private soldier mistaking an order to fall back, lest they should be outflanked by the enemy, for a command to retreat, ran through the lines, crying at the top of his voice, *retreat, retreat.* This produced an immediate confusion. The man was alarmed himself and communicated his feelings to others. They were struck; were palsied in their efforts; supposed it an order from the commanding officer, but knew not why it was given, nor what to make of it. But it had a disheartening effect which increased till it grew into a panic, and they began to scatter and run hither and thither. The officers used their utmost efforts ta rally them, but to no purpose. Mr. Franklin, who acted as lieutenant, ran backwards and forwards, calling upon the men to stand; but they had begun to fly, terror had seized them, and they were no longer masters of themselves.— The Indians quickly saw their confusion, rallied, rushed out of the woods, naked, yelling like furies, tomahawk in hand, carrying terror to the hearts of those who, ten minutes before, defied and drove them. It had now become almost a complete rout, the men flying for their lives like a herd of frighted cattle, and the Indians, like hungry wolves, leaping out upon them. Many were killed with the tomahawk; others were shot down in their flight; and of that gallant band who marched out fresh and strong in the morning full of life and health, probably not more than forty or fifty escaped. The rest were mangled corpses.

Lieut. Franklin having done all he could to repair the disasters of the day, and worn out with excessive fatigues, was constrained to leave the ground. His commanding officer, Col. Dorrance, told him nothing more could be done, and every man would have to look out for himself. He walked away slowly from the ground, loaded his piece, turned and fired upon his pursuers, loaded and fired as he went, and laid his course for the river. It was hardly possible that he could reach it alive, for there was an open flat which he would have to cross, in full view of the enemy, where they might either shoot him, or cut him down with the hatchet, as they had done many others. To escape was his first object, and if he could not, his purpose was to sell his life at a high price; for he had repeatedly declared he never would be taken alive by the Indians. Immediately before him was a bank, (not the bank of the river) at the foot of which ran a little brook with alder and hazle bushes growing thickly on both sides of it. It was a close thicket. Beyond this spot was an open field extending to the river. When he came to the bank, and was passing down, he turned his head and saw no enemy watching him at the moment, and having no time to load regularly, he poured powder out of his horn into the muzzle of his gun, and dropped in after it two balls which he had carried in his mouth all day. Having done this in less time than I occupy in telling it, he threw himself into the thicket of alders or hazles upon his face, drawing his gun close to his side, and there lay in a dreadful state of suspense, not knowing but that the murderous hatchet would be sunk into his head at the next breath he might attempt to draw. He lay like one dead, with suppressed breathing, not daring to make the least motion lest the enemy might see or hear him. His position did not permit him to see, but he could hear, and *did* hear the footsteps of his deadly foes, and knew that they passed by very near to him. It was not more than a minute or two after he threw himself into the bushes, before the Indians rushed by and overtook his captain, with whom he had just been conversing, and butchered him without mercy. So near was this to where he lay that he could hear him speak and ask for quarter; and every stroke of the horrid tomahawk as they struck it, blow after blow, into the head and body of his expiring friend, sounded into his ears. He could hear his dying groans, and the heavy gurgling in his throat as he drew his breath with difficulty through the flowing blood with which he was nearly strangled. These dying groans of his neighbor fell heavily upon his ear and heart, and seemed to toll his own death-knell; for he hardly expected to escape. Yet he was spared, shielded by the protecting care of him who governs all things, and without whom not a sparrow falls to the ground.

He supposed, as he afterwards stated, that the enemy must have seen him, but imagined him dead, and being in hot pursuit of the fugitives, did not stop to examine him. It was near sunset when he threw himself into the bush, and he lay still, without stirring hand or foot, till it began to grow dark He listened, and listened again, and could hear nothing save the heavy breathing of the dying officer. The noise and confusion and heat of the day, had given place to the cool shadows and solemn stillness of the evening. He ventured to raise his head slowly and look about him. The enemy had left the field. He rose and stood upon his feet. His first care was to examine his gun. The barrel was nearly half full of powder He loaded it aright and then started for the fort, keeping a good look out. No enemy was to be seen or heard, and as he went onward, he acquired confidence of safety. He arrived at the fort and found it filled with women and children, who set up a loud wailing when they saw him, being reminded of their loss, and unable to contain the grief which rent their bosoms. They surrounded him; they seized him by the hand; they cried out, "Have you seen my husband?" "Have you seen my father?" "Have you seen my brother?" It was more than he could bear. He could stand the shock of battle, but this scene overpowered him. He spoke to them kindly, and endeavored to hush the noise of their grief, and succeeded in some measure, but the deep heavy sobs of inward anguish which broke from them when they tried to suppress their feelings, went to his heart, and he soon hurried away from a place where he witnessed sorrows too great to be quieted by man. He turned and went to his house. It was deserted, and he found himself a solitary wanderer at his own door. His wife had heard the news of the victory gained by the British and Indians, with such trrrible slaughter of the Americans, and fearing that her husband was killed, made her escape with her family down the river, in a boat. It was now a time of mourning, wailing and woe. Desolation reigned universally, and the voice of rejoiceing was no longer heard in the valley of Wyoming. Wives and mothers who, twenty four hours since, felt themselves rich and strong in husbands and sons, now uttered tones of distress, and shed tears of bitter grief, on account of their irreparable loss. The affliction was universal. Not a family but had lost a husband, son, or brother, or some near friend. It seemed as if the Lord had a controversy with that people, and had determined that they should be sorely tried, that they might be led to review their ways and repent of their sins.

The slaughter was very sore after the fatal retreat began, and it is supposed that, of the hundreds of brave men, who went out with courage and confidence in the morning, to beat back their invaders, not more than one in eight remained alive to tell the sad story of their defeat; and a portion of these escaped almost by miracle. The excessive heat of the sun caused an exhaustion and faintness in some, which made them a more easy prey to the enemy. On the whole, the disappointed hopes and fatal disasters of the day were such that they could neither be easily repaired, nor soon forgotten. Indeed, the sudden loss of so many dear relatives could never be made up to the survivors by any thing earthly. None but God could bind up those hearts, torn by so sudden and violent a dismemberment, from objects dear to them as life. Oh, war! war! what destruction and misery follow in thy train! When will the time come when the nations shall learn to live in peace; when every man shall be deemed a brother; and when all shall seek the happiness of all with a brother's heart.

CHAPTER III.

Flight of the Franklins down the river—They have the small pox—Their return the next spring to their former residence—Loss of their eldest son by the Indians—Capture and return of the second and his cousin.

In the preceding chapter I mentioned the fact that Mrs. Franklin, fearing that her husband was killed, fled for her life, down the river. It was the night following the day of the battle. I will give the particulars of it. Mr. Franklin owned a boat which he had employed in the shad fishery, and before he went out to the fight, charged his wife to take care of it, lest in case of disaster, others should seize it and she be left without any means of escape.

The counsel was wise, for no man could tell beforehand what would be the result of the action; as the events of war often mock all human calculation. Mrs. Franklin followed the advice which her husband gave her, and found it, indeed, necessary to her safety to do so, for others, as well as herself, having to fly for their lives, would have taken the boat and gone down the river with it, if she had been at all negligent of her charge. One, and another, and another, came to take possession of it, but she stood there and held the chain in her hand, and refused to let it go, waiting to see if her husband would not return from battle. She kept her post of fatigue and danger several hours. She tarried late, but no husband came, no glad news of victory sounded in her ears. but heavy tidings of slaughter and defeat, and ruin to her cause, came pouring in upon her. She felt that she could no longer remain with safety, and hurried on board with her six children. Five other women, with their families, accompanied her in the same boat. Two of the husbands of these women came in, in the course of the night, having escaped from the field of battle, and brought word to her that they supposed her husband was killed. It was a heavy stroke, but she had no leisure to sit down and mourn. Though almost dead with anxiety and fatigue, she had six young children looking up to her for help, and it behooved her to put every nerve and muscle into action for their support, and this kept her from sinking. She must live and act for her children. If she yielded to despondency, what would they do? What would become of them? No, she would not yield; a mother's heart sustained her. God, who knew what she could bear, and would not suffer her to be crushed, was merciful to her. They started from Nanticoke flats, where they then lived, and reached the fall, or rapids, a short distance below, and there lay by and waited till daylight should enable them to pass down in safety. The next day they went over the falls without any accident or damage. Here Mrs. Franklin experienced a happy relief from one severe portion of her burdens. Her husband, whom she had been led almost to despair of ever seeing again alive, overtook them at this place. It was a happiness, indeed, to see his face once more, almost as one risen from the dead, and to hear his courageous voice exerted to encourage and strengthen the little worn out and dispirited party. It was not only her *husband* whom she saw alive, it was the *man* who had risked his life for her and her children, and friends; who left not the field of battle till the very last; and who had been exposed to a hundred deaths, who now stood before her; and no wonder if she felt more than words can express. The first emotions of the meeting being over, he proceeded to give them his advice. He bade them not to be in a hurry to go, for the ground was entirely cleared of the Indians, who, he said, would find enough to do where they were, at present, and would not be at all likely to pursue after them. He found fault with the men whom he overtook, and reproved them for being in such a hurry to get away, and said he thought they ought to use some reason and judgment in such a case, and not go off and leave things to be wasted and destroyed. He returned the same day and a neighbor with him, to their place of residence, it was not far, and carried out of his house things which would be wanted, principally articles of iron ware, and hid them. This he did to secure them from being stolen by the Indians, who might return, and plunder the house in his absence. Having safely deposited his wares where he could find them again, he went back to his family. Thence they floated down the river to an Irish settlement, several miles below, where they procured a shelter. This being accomplished, he went up the river again to secure his harvest. By extraordinary exertions his grain was taken care of in the course of a few weeks. He hastened the more because it was a hazardous business. For aught he knew to the contrary, the enemy might have returned by this time, and might be lurking about the premises, ready to shoot down and scalp every comer. By the good providence of God he was not molested. While he was gone the family had the small pox the natural way, and some of them very severely. One of the daughters died. The names of the children were Joseph, Olive, Roswell, Susannah, Thankful and Stephen. Thankful died, and Stephen had the disease to such a degree, producing such malignant sores, that he was crippled in his arms ever after; not wholly unable to labor, but unfit for heavy work.

While all had the small pox together, it was mercifully ordered that Olive had it in so mild a form as to be able to be about the house and wait upon the rest all the time, with the exception of two or three hours, when she was sick with the symptoms. She was only eleven years of age, but having good resolution, and seeing the situation of the others, and feeling the necessity of the case, she exerted herself to good purpose for their relief. It was a time of real distress with them; all sick, and only one little girl to take care of them. And what made their sufferings the more severe was, they were not permitted to go abroad to any of the neighbors, and had to be crowded together in the loft of a little spring-house, in the lower part of which the Irish family of whom they hired it, were accustomed to set their milk. This close place, under a thin shingle roof, in the month of July, was like a heated oven in the afternoons. Here having to lie, and swelter and pant in their weakness, under such a burning heat, it is not to be wondered at that some of them should die; the wonder is, that any of them survived. After an absence of some weeks, Mr. Franklin returned and found his family still afflicted with the terrible disease, and submitted to inoculation. He passed through it well; having no trouble, except with the symptoms, and was soon able to attend to business as usual. On account of the long continued ill health of some of the family, and the lateness of the season before they could be ready to go, and the unsettled state of the country, it was judged expedient to spend the winter in the vicinity of the place where they now were, and not attempt to go up the river till the ensuing spring. In the spring they returned to their former place of residence. A little grain had been secured during the previous summer, but all their cattle had been driven off by the Indians and Tories, and they were in a very destitute condition. Previous to this, Mr. Franklin had been up the river to Nanticoke, with his eldest son Joseph, to make some preparation for his family, before he should bring them on, and having completed his design returned, leaving Joseph with one of the neighbors. He supposed it safe to do so, as no Indians were on the ground, or near it, that he knew of, and he hop-

ed, when he came back with the other members of
his household, to find his eldest son there ready to
welcome and receive them. They came, but found
no Joseph on the ground to greet them with a smile.
Alas, the lad was gone they knew not whither, and
they never saw his face again. They supposed,
at the time, that he was taken by the Indians, and
they afterwards learned the fact, and some particulars about it. It seems that a party of Indians
made an attack upon the house where Joseph was
left, and killed the man and carried off the woman
and her children. There were only two or three
families then on the ground, and the enemy, according to their custom, came secretly upon them, and
gave them no chance either for defence or escape.
Joseph, unwilling to be captured, made an attempt
to get away, and had some prospect of it, but failed
of success. He ran for a canoe which lay in the
river, near by. His life was at stake, and he made
all possible haste. Fear was behind him, and hope
beckoned him forward. He almost cleared his distance, and seemed on the point of complete deliverance. But just at this instant two Indians in advance of the rest, and nearer the river, hailed him
and commanded him to stop. He heeded them not;
his soul was up; he flew rather than ran, and a
few leaps more would have brought him to his object, when a cruel shot from the enemy arrested
him. He was wounded in the thigh and could run
no further. Alas, poor young man! the dewy
brightness of his morning was darkened by a cloud,
and never shone again. To him no sun arose to

light him along the path of virtue, industry and competence in this world. What he might have been, if he had lived, cannot be known. The Great Author of his being saw fit to give him an early dismission from this life. It was wisely ordered no doubt, and there we leave it. He was found, the next day, to be too sore to travel on foot, and keep up with the party. The others went on, but he, and the two Indians who took him, remained behind. When they afterwards came up with their company, Joseph was not with them, and they had a fresh scalp. His fate cannot be doubted.

This account was received from Mrs. Lester, at whose house he was left, whose husband the Indians shot, and took her and her children prisoners and carried them away to Canada She afterwards returned from her captivity and became Mr. Franklin's second wife, and is now living with her youngest daughter, Mrs. Benedict, near Brockport, on the Hudson and Erie Canal, in the 98th year of her age.

The disappointment and grief of the family, upon their arrival at their old place of residence, to find it altogether lonely and deserted, their neighbors killed or swept into captivity, their dear son and brother gone, and none to tell them any thing which could dispel their doubts and anxieties, may be felt by those who have suffered sudden and distressing losses of friends, but can scarcely be realized by others. What to make of it, or what had become of them, they could not tell at first. They continued not long in suspense. They found one of the neighbors, named Hagerman, who had been badly wounded. and was probably supposed to be dead, or nearly so, but who afterwards revived and crept into the bushes and hid himself, and thus evaded the grasp of his foes. He gave them a history of the distressing affair which, although it afforded them not much comfort, relieved them from some portion of the darkness which had hung upon their minds.

It might be hoped that this family would now be permitted to enjoy a season of rest and prosperity, after so many reverses, and that their peace and domestic comforts would, for a time, remain undisturbed. But war was abroad in the land, and the frontiers were continually exposed to the sudden and secret incursions of the Indians. These subtle foes would lurk for days and weeks in the woods, on the hills, whence they could look off and discern the movements of the settlers who lived on the flats, and when they thought them unprepared, would dart upon them, and plunder, and burn, and kill, and carry off prisoners, a family at a time, or more, or fewer, just as circumstances admitted.— Such being the state of things, safety and comfort were scarcely to be thought of, much less to be expected. It was a time of alarms and changes, and this family seems to have had its full share in the calamities which, in those days of trouble, came upon the people.

Their next sore affliction consisted in the capture, by the Indians, of the second son, Roswell, and a cousin of his, who was in company with him. I shall give the account as I took it down from his own mouth. He lives now near the village of Aurora, in the county of Cayuga, a humble disciple of the Lord Jesus, blessed with competence, and spared to a good old age, being near 70. The cousin's name, who was taken with him, was Arnold Franklin, whose father fell in the battle of Wyoming, and who came to live with his uncle about the time Joseph was taken and killed. Before Roswell and Arnold fell into the hands of the Indians, the family had moved from Nanticoke to Solomon's Creek, up the river about three miles, near to a block house, erected for the defence of the settlers against the incursions of the Tories and Indians. The boys started to go from this block house to Nanticoke. Certain Indians lay concealed in the bushes, by the road side, to seize upon the defenceless, or shoot them down as they were passing by. They had been hanging round, as they afterwards stated, several days, upon the hills, watching for an opportunity to leap upon their prey and carry it off to a place of safety. Now was their chance, and they improved it. They seized the lads, and as they were unarmed, forebore to fire upon them. Soon after they were made prisoners, the Indians fired upon a man, Mr. Corey, who was very near being taken by them, but escaped, after they fired upon him, by taking a different route from the one they expected. He left the road he was in when they fired at him, crossed a creek, made his way through the bushes and got off in safety. The boys were on their way to the farm, to commence ploughing, at the time they were captured, and the Indians went right on with them to the same place. When they arrived they found the Indians had taken six horses, three of which belonged to Mr. Franklin. The boys were placed upon two of the horses, and a squaw, wife of one of the party, was seated upon a third. Three others of the red men mounted the other three horses, and onward they moved through the wilderness, toward an Indian village, in the Genesee country. There were twenty men in the party, and when those who were on horseback set forward, seventeen were left behind. The boys, and those who were with them, suffered extremely, during some part of their journey, from hunger. They were at one time nearly five days without any thing to eat, except nuts and berries, which they found in the woods. Before the five days were quite ended, they came across an old bear and her two cubs. They killed the old bear first, and then shot the cubs, who had climbed a tree to get out of the reach of their pursuers. But in vain; the bullets of their enemies brought them, one after the other, tumbling down to the ground. As long as their bear meat lasted they had provisions in plenty. This did not afford to them, however, a sufficient supply for the whole of their journey. They made out to live, some how or other; and at last, after many hardships, reached an Indian village, where they continued till the remainder of the party came in. These last brought in five prisoners and two scalps, and all, soon after, set out for fort Niagara. And here it may be proper to notice a custom which prevailed among the Indians, always when prisoners were brought in. Those who brought them made it their business to give notice of the fact, by a peculiar yell, whenever they approached an Indian village. This yell, more shrill and stirring than the martial fife and drum, never failed to summon together, in an instant, as if by magic, all the Indians within hearing, old and young, men, women and children.— As soon as the prisoners came within reach, every one gave them a cut with a stick, club, or fist, or whatever else they happened to have in hand, no matter what, and the more it hurt the greater the fun. Mr. Franklin says that he expected to be killed, and actually was almost pounded to death the first time he run the gauntlet. He was, at the time, separate from the other prisoners, and understood not how the thing was managed. Afterwards, when he had learned their play, he looked out better, and avoided many a hard knock. The prisoners were kept moving forward, and made progress, notwithstanding occasional delays, and arrived finally, at fort Niagara, where they were delivered up to the British. The two boys were appointed to be waiters to two British officers, and remained there through the winter. In the spring, Roswell went to the Genesee river, as waiter to an American, who had joined the king's troops. He spent a considerable space of time, (several months in the whole,) at different villages, but stayed longer at Caneadea, than at any other place. During this period the Indians held a great dance at Cane-adea, on the Genesee river, above Nunda falls.— To raise their zeal to a more furious pitch of excitement, they procured a keg of ardent spirits.— The women, well knowing the horrid, murderous work, which the infernal stuff would make among their husbands, fathers and brothers, carefully gathered up all the instruments of death, and hid them, before the ceremonies began. This is their uniform custom, and it is a matter of great importance that it should be attended to, for the poor creatures when set on fire by rum or whiskey, are fully prepared to fight, and even to butcher one another in the most savage manner, without any sense of the tremendous criminality of such doings. Such is the effect of intoxicating drinks upon Indians, and not upon them only. How many murders among white people may be traced to the same source. Some, by their habits of drinking, are turned into fools, others become brutes, and others again are transformed into furious madmen. And in some instances, the same individual passes through all these stages of vile self-destruction, until in the end, he becomes a scorched, crippled and loathsome lump of wretchedness. The wise and safe course is, not to partake of the intoxicating cup at all. To use it as a beverage or treat, is neither right nor safe, and all who sell the article for the purpose of being turned down the throats of men, if not drunkards themselves, help to make others so, and many of them fall, at last, into the same ditch which they helped to dig for their fellow men.

For such persons no excuse can be made at the present day, after so much light has been thrown upon the subject. Their guilt must be great, and their account awful. Men may uphold them, but God will bring them down. And what must we think concerning those unprincipled wretches who make it their business, first to get the Indians drunk, and then to cheat them in trade, and wrong them out of their property, or out of money due to them from the government? Men who know better, and employ their superior light, not to elevate and bless the sons of the forest, but to corrupt and degrade them for the sake of filthy lucre, cannot be excused. They are the genuine disciples of Judas, and must share the same awful doom, except they repent.

About the time of this famous dance, Roswell seemed upon the point of losing his life. The circumstances were these. A certain Indian, a noted warrior, passing through Caneadea, called to see Col. or Capt. Johnson, a British officer, who lived here among the Indians, at the time. Johnson had gone away, and had left Roswell alone, in charge of the house. The warrior came, and enquired for Johnson, and was told he was not at home. He knew that there was a supply of spirits about the premises, but did not know where it was kept.— He moved his eyes carefully round the room, as if to search every spot, and finally settled them, with a severe and scrutinizing glare, upon the lad, but said not a word. Roswell did not move, nor show any signs of moving, but sat as if nailed to the spot. The warrior drew his long, sharp knife, seized him by the head, and with a most ferocious look, brandished the weapon as if he meant to plunge it into his bosom. It was a dreadful moment to poor Roswell, who expected to be butchered upon the spot, but made no outcry, and offered no resistance. The Indian presently let him go, after giving him two or three hard thumps upon the head with his knuckles. It was a most happy relief and a great mercy to escape thus, without a wound, from the hand of a fierce savage, disappointed and angered by a boy in a point where the demands of appetite were so loud. Why he did not kill him is not known. It might be owing to his perfect silence and non-resistance, and to his showing no symptoms of fear or anger. Perhaps also the Indian might have been restrained by a regard for the officer under whose protection the boy was placed. Whatever might have been the second causes, God was his preserver. This, among many other mercies, is a subject of thanksgiving not to be forgotten in old age, by one who was thus mercifully spared in the days of his youth.

In the spring of 1781, Roswell returned to fort Niagara, where an exchange of prisoners soon began to be talked of. When he and his cousin found that the names of those who wanted to go were being taken down, they procured their names to be set down among the number. Some individuals, for reasons best known to themselves, chose to stay. To the two lads, and to many others, the hope of seeing home and friends once more, would have been sufficient inducement to draw them away from their present situation, if it had been ten times as inviting as it was. For the sake of home, they were ready to encounter cheerfully every difficulty which might lie in their path. They cared not for hardships if they might but see again the faces of those whom they dearly loved. When the British had collected their prisoners together, to the amount of about thirty in number, they put them aboard a vessel and sailed with them to Carlton Island.— There they landed, and went thence to Montreal in boats. In this city they remained several months; were kept in the provost jail; had the liberty of a small yard, and were supplied with plenty of provisions.

When the time for their liberation came, the prisoners were ferried across the St. Lawrence. Thence they went to the outlet of Lake Champlain. Thence up the Lake by water to Ticonderoga. There they tarried several days, waiting the arrival of an officer, on the part of the Americans, to whom word had been sent by the British, with the understanding that there would be an exchange of prisoners at this time. The officer, at length, made his appearance, and took charge of them. The two boys, and some of the other prisoners, were in earnest to go ahead, and procured a boat and rowed all night, and arrived at Skeensborough in the morning. There were five boys in the company; Roswell and his cousin, and three Kentuckians.— They obtained a pass at some place on the road;

sold their blanket coats; procured a little money, and traveled together, on foot, to Albany. There they found a chance to be conveyed some distance down the river by water. After which they had to leave the water, and travel on foot, as far as Esopus. There they parted: the Kentuckians going one course, and the two cousins another. Roswell and his fellow traveller left the river, and passing through Minisink, directed their steps toward the much desired valley of Wyoming. They travelled all the way on foot, with the exception of a chance ride, very rarely, for no great distance. It was hard work for limbs so young, but the hope of seeing those they loved made them bear it bravely. After some days of wearisome travel, they came in sight of the old and well remembered place. It was a welcome sight; it was a spot dear to their hearts. There had been some change; the house was different; but they heeded it not; the mountains, the forests, the fields, the river, all the great features of nature remained unaltered. They stepped softly, and with light hearts, up to the door of the house where they expected to find their dear kindred. Roswell entered the house and saw his father. His cousin entered with him. They found the old man seated within, in a musing posture.— He was struck, for he had not heard whether they were dead or alive, and was not in the least expecting to see them at that time. Their sudden appearance, as they silently entered the room and he caught a glimpse of their faces, quite overcame him. His feelings were too full to permit him to speak.

It was a solemn pause. After his emotions had found vent, and some moments of silent thought had passed away, he was able to command sufficient strength to converse freely. The father has been mentioned, the mother was not there, and the afflicted son was never more to see her face in this world. He had to learn now, for the first time, what had become of her. A subsequent part of this narrative will inform the reader. It may well be supposed that the two lads had much to hear, and much to say. What their conversation was, how many questions were asked and answered, what tides of feeling moved through their bosoms, may be imagined by those who have been in like situations, but cannot well be made plain and interesting to others. To them it was happiness enough for one day, that the privations, toils and perils of their captivity were ended; that the welcome of dear friends was warm and fresh upon their hearts; and that nothing of their past sufferings remained, except such a remembrance of them as would serve to increase their present joys. One subject of grief, the loss of a dear mother, was present, indeed, to their minds, but this, while it served to soften their hearts, did not take away their happiness. It caused a more solemn and tender feeling. It reminded them of many things which she had said and done while living. And although her face was hidden from their view, her image was often present before their imagination, and precious in their thoughts. She had been dear to them, and to all the family, but God had taken her away, and *he* had done right in it, and it behooved them all to be satisfied with his dealings in the matter, and thankful also that so many of them had been spared, and were now so happily brought together.

CHAPTER IV.

The mother and four children taken prisoners by the Indians—Pursued by the whites—A skirmish—Mrs. Franklin killed—The youngest child carried off—The others recovered.

Having gone through the account of the capture and return of Roswell Franklin and his cousin, the next subject in the order of events, relates to the seizure of the family by the Indians, who hurried them away into the wilderness before help could be obtained to prevent it. I shall give the narrative as I took it down from the mouth of Mrs. Olive Stevens, now in the 72d year of her age, then a little girl of thirteen. Though so far advanced in years, she still retains, through the goodness of God, a good measure of health and strength, and the possession, very little impaired, of all her powers of mind. The members of the family taken prisoners at this time with Olive, were her mother, not far from —— years of age, her sister Susannah eleven, her brother Stephen four, and Ichabod a year and six months. They were captured on the 8th of April, in the year 1781. It was on the Lord's day about noon, when Mrs. Franklin, wishing to prepare dinner for her family, sent one of her little daughters to a spring, not far distant, to procure some water. There were bushes around the spring, behind which persons might lurk and keep themselves hidden from the sight of those who came for water. The little girl approached the spot, not thinking what these bushes contained, or what was so soon to befal herself. The Indians were there and seized her. It was done without noise, and in a moment, and no noise was made by her. She did not dare to make an outcry. Mr. Franklin was out of the house at this time, having gone abroad into the fields and woods to look for one of his swine which was missing. The child did not return to the house and they called her, but received no answer. Again, and again they sounded her name, but in vain, all was silent. Mrs. Franklin and Olive were at the house, and began to fear that the Indians were lying in ambush near the spring, and had taken her prisoner. They were not left long in suspense. The first we knew, says Mrs. Stevens, (Olive,) the door was pushed open, and eight guns were pointed right in upon us. Here were eight Indians ready to rush in upon one defenceless woman and her little ones.—There was no chance to hide or run; they were completely in the power of their enemies, who seeing no man within, took possession of the house as their own, and gave every one of the inmates a thump with the fist, as much as to say, you belong to us, you must do as we say. They then went to plundering and dashing about as hard as they could. They soon dispatched what they dared to do, (for it was mid-day and they might be subject to unpleasant interruption,) and hurried the family off out of the way of discovery and pursuit. In the hurry of the moment Olive started without her shoes, but the rough ground soon caused her to feel the need of them, and she pointed to her feet, and made the Indians understand that she could not travel without them. They permitted her to return to the house for her shoes, which she had left under a bed. She saw that they had put a shovel full of live coals into a feather bed, and a pillow upon the coals to burn the house, but she did not dare to extinguish the fire, for two of the Indians came back with her, and were at the door, prepared to watch all her motions. Having procured her shoes, she felt able to travel with the best of them. The whole party started for a hill at no great distance, and climbed to the top of it. The Indians carried the small children, or at least the infant, and Olive and her mother, and Susannah, went on foot. When they had reached the top of the ridge they could see Wilksbarre, and hear the cannon firing an alarm, as they supposed, to rouse the inhabitants into a pursuit of the Indians, and could also see the smoke of their house ascending before their eyes, as a melancholy token of their lately happy, but now utterly desolate state. It is not easy, perhaps, for us to enter into a full view of the loneliness of their feelings, as they saw their once loved and still tenderly regretted home consuming to ashes, and more especially, as they felt themselves in a wilderness, in the hands of wandering savages, who might carry them off a great distance, they knew not whither, perhaps never to return. Were we to sit down at a short distance and see our own house and furniture burning up, without any power to stop the flame, the sight would probably make us sad, but we should still have kind friends around us, ready to sympathize with us, and to put forth a helping hand to our relief. But what if we were in the hands of Indians, carrying us and our little children into the woods, hastening us away from every earthly friend and helper, what would be our emotions in such a case? Would we not soon cease to regard our house and goods? and would not our trouble be—what will become of me and my children? Let the house burn, if our lives may only be spared.

Not long after the party had gone and carried away his family, Mr. Franklin returned. He found his house on fire, and the roof just ready to fall in. Though he had been accustomed to so many reverses, he felt, nevertheless, almost overpowered by this. It came unexpectedly; it had fallen suddenly; it was a most sweeping stroke. Hitherto he had lost but a child or two at a time, now his wife and most of his children were swept at once into captivity, or destroyed by fire, for at first, he was uncertain which. He searched diligently about the premises in every direction and found, ere long, two guns, one or both of which he had previously won from his savage foes, in some of his rencounters with them. These the party had taken from his house, and having broken them off at the lock, by striking them against a stump, had gone and left them. He noticed also the tracks which were made, and the next day, stirred up the ashes of his house to ascertain whether there were any bones among them, and on the whole, became fully confirmed in the opinion he had formed the preceding day; to wit, that the Indians had carried off his dear companion and her helpless flock, his own beloved children, into the wide howling wilderness. It would not have been strange, if like David and his men, when the Amalekites had plundered and burnt Ziklag, and carried off their wives, and their sons, and their daughters, "he had lifted up his voice and wept till he had no more power to weep." (see 1 Sam. 30. 3, 4.) He had cause for grief; his family was taken away, and he was left alone. He had reason also to reflect, and seriously to enquire, why it was that the dear objects of his affection should become the prey of wolfish men, and he be spared. He was the object dreaded and hated by his foes, and why had they not waylaid and shot him ere this? He might think of it, and ponder also upon the narrow escape which he had just made, by being away from the house, at the time it was taken and burnt. It was a providential deliverance; a new instance added to those which had gone before, of the watchful care of the Lord over him. That he should evade the blow aimed at him at this time, is the more remarkable from the fact, that the Indians had been lurking about, and watching for an opportunity to kill or take him and others for several days. This fact one of them who could talk English related to the family, after they had been with them a day or two, as prisoners.— The account, in substance, is this. The Indians lay in ambush, near the spot where Mr. Franklin was preparing the timber for putting up a sawmill. They kept themselves concealed in a grove of hemlocks, on a rising ground, where they could plainly see and hear the white people at their work, but could not be discovered by them. Their calculation was to fire upon them when they were engaged in the act of raising the mill, expecting to shoot down some of them, to have the frame fall upon others, and kill or maim them, and to throw the remainder into confusion, and thus win a complete and easy victory. Their plan was well laid, and had fair promise of entire success, but was frustrated by the following means. On the very day of the raising, while the Indians lay watching, as the Panther eyes his intended victim before he leaps upon him, they saw, to their confusion, about a dozen armed men approach the spot, well prepared to defend themselves and their companions. These men came from the Shawney village or settlement, several miles distant, down the river, having been, some time before, invited to attend and bring their guns with them. The other men, who lived in the vicinity, not apprehending any danger, came without their arms, and would have been utterly routed by the execution of the well devised scheme of their enemies, if it had not been for the defence thus opportunely, through the goodness of

God, provided for them. The mill was raised without interruption. The armed men returned with Mr. Franklin to his house for supper, and the Indians saw them go in. They did not leave the house till after dark, and the enemy, not knowing when they went, imagined that they tarried all night. This saved the family; for had the Indians known their defenceless state they would have attacked the house that night, and Mr. Franklin would probably have been killed; for he had made a firm resolve never to be taken by them alive.— And others of the household, in the heat and confusion of a night attack, might have been sorely wounded or slaughtered. Thus the enemy were kept back by fear, and the inmates of the house slept quietly, not having the slightest suspicion of the extreme danger to which they were exposed.

We left Mrs. Franklin and her children in the hands of their enemies, standing on a rising ground, whence they could see Wilksbarre, and where the smoke of their humble dwelling was distinctly visible; let us return to them again. Having taken their last, long, lingering look of home, and of the hills, and flats, and fields, well known to them, they went on their way. The party consisted of Mrs. Franklin, her daughter Olive, in her 14th year, and three other children still younger, as before mentioned, and eight Indians. They encamped the first night in a thick swamp, where they kindled a small fire. Within a short distance from their camp was a run, to which they went for water. Here a fair opening for an escape was presented before the mind of Olive. She could see by the dim light of the fire what course to take, thought of attempting it, and hoped, under the cover of the night, to be able to effect it. The distance from the settlements of the white people was not great, and she might possibly have reached them before her pursuers could have overtaken her. But remembering to have heard that if a part of their prisoners left them, it was the Indian custom to put the rest to death, she feared to go, lest the family should lose their lives on that account. She encouraged herself also to remain where she was, with the hope that the white people would follow on and rescue them. The next day they labored onward, with great difficulty, through a thick laurel swamp, to the spot where five of the party were left, when they were on their way to the white settlements, on account of the lameness or illness of one or two of them. The trouble and fatigue of making their way through such tangled thickets, and through so much mud and water, can scarcely be conceived by those who have not tried it. When the two parties, the eight who went, and the five who stayed, met again, they held a talk and divided their prisoners. They took my mother and gave her to one and said, this is yours; me, says Mrs. Stevens, they bestowed upon another, my sister, brother, and the child they allotted to others. Every one had a separate master.

The third day of their captivity, they travelled through some part of the great swamp which lies east of Wilksbarre, between the Susquehannah and

Delaware rivers. In the course of the day they had to cross a road, and the Indians required them to step from one stone to another, so as to make no tracks. They were evidently afraid of pursuers. In the course of the day the life of Stephen, then about four years old, was threatened; or there seemed a probability of its being taken away by those who had him in their keeping. He had sores on his legs, caused by the small pox, and the Indians were afraid of taking it from him. They were told that the time had passed away when he was capable of communicating it to others, but they did not appear satisfied. One of them was seen whetting a knife, who afterwards, in company with another, took Stephen and carried him away out of sight. His mother mournfully exclaimed, "we shall never see Stephen again." It really appeared as if they actually intended to take his life. To the great joy, however, of the afflicted family, he was brought back to the encampment, at night, alive.— On the fourth day, Wednesday, they were nearly or quite destitute of provisions. The Indians took some articles of food from the house when they burnt it, but these were now expended. On Thursday they had nothing to feed upon but wintergreens; and nothing on Friday, till toward the latter part of the day, when they shot two or three black squirrels and caught a few little fish. Some time on Friday they stopped on a narrow flat near the Susquehannah, where they kindled two little fires, and seemed inclined to stay over night, but soon changed their minds and passed on. About this time two of the party, who had been absent the night before, returned. Mrs. Franklin and the children observed them very busily engaged in conversing together, and afterwards saw them put out their fires, and imagined they did it through fear of their enemies. Presently one of them who could talk English said, "rebels after us," and pointing to the top of the hill said, "Yankees up there." They packed up their matters and went along the side of the hill, and when they stopped for the night, did not encamp in a body, but lay scattered here and there, and abstained from shooting. They also went out of their direct route, for the purpose of evading pursuit. They came finally to the Wylusing creek, where they passed the night. Here their fish and squirrels were boiled in water. The Indians gave their prisoners the water in which the fish were boiled for drink, and a quarter of a squirrel each, to eat; and it was, says Mrs. Stevens, the best victuals I ever tasted. The Indian who claimed Stephen wanted to have him sleep in the same blanket with him, but the boy resolutely refused, and could not be made to submit to his wishes. This irritated him, and he hit the child a cuff with his fist and let him go, and he went and slept with his mother. The Indians laughed.

Saturday morning. The party was slow about starting; they were out of provisions, and seemed to be in a study to know what to do. The little ones became uneasy. Susannah cried. She and Stephen could not bear to be carried by the Indians. Finally, it was agreed among them to carry the infant, and let the others travel on foot. The humanity of these red men toward the little children on this, and on other occasions, is worthy of commendation, and places them far above many of those pale faced savages who pretend to be so much their superiors. They went on their way moderately, and before noon made a halt. After resting a while the Indians began to look carefully round, and peep through the oak bushes which covered the hill. Mrs. Franklin imagined that they were looking out for deer, and that the deer were not far off. Soon they began to hear the report of guns, and found that there was something besides deer among the bushes. White men were there in pursuit of Indians. The foes saw each other, and were on the alert to seize every advantage which might present itself in their favor. The poor afflicted mother, and her dear little ones, lay right between the combatants, and heard their bullets whistle through the air. It was not a time for them to rest, or to feel at their ease. They could hear every gun that was fired, and every shout that was uttered. The white men nicknamed the Indians "copperheads," and they called the whites "rebels." These opprobrious epithets they could hear the parties fling out against each other as they were about to shoot. First the loud yell, "copperhead"—"rebel," next the roar of the musket and the whiz of the bullet. In the midst of this wild, woods fight, the family rose and stood up and listened. An Indian came along and told them to lie down, or they would be killed. The mother was wounded already. As to herself, Mrs. Sevens says, "she felt no fear of the battle, or of the bullets which whistled by, nor had she the least dread of the Indians all the time she was with them, after the first fright." She says, "she does not know but that the greatness of the first alarm drove all fear out of her, for she felt none afterwards."

She thinks, from what she remembers to have heard, that there were six Indians killed in this skirmish. One she saw fall during the action.

The affair took place on Saturday afternoon, the 15th of April, the 7th day after they were taken. The fight was in the bushes, and was close, desultory and hot. To show a little the spirit which then prevailed, I will mention the following incident, as given by Mrs. Stevens. One Taylor, a man belonging to the pursuing party, shot an Indian doctor, tried to scalp him, and broke his knife in the attempt. Two Indians were seen coming toward him, and some of his company loudly warned him of his danger, and told him to run, or they would be upon him and take his life. But he was not to be diverted from his purpose; he declared he would have the scalp; and being hurried in the business, and not very expert at it, he cut off the head and ran away with it, and escaped unhurt. The white people drove the Indians and became masters of the ground. After the firing ceased, Mrs. Franklin, anxious to know whether her husband was there, raised herself up upon her elbow to look.— She directed her attention toward the white people, up the hill above them. Her daughter Susannah meanwhile turned her eyes the other way, and saw an Indian approach, and said, "mother lie down, there is an Indian coming, and he will kill you." The words were scarcely out of the child's mouth before her prediction was fulfilled. The fatal bullet pierced her back, between her shoulders, and she sunk down mortally wounded. She fell upon her daughter Olive, who lay partly behind her and spoke to her, but received no answer. Her mother rolled up her eyes as if she wanted to speak, but said nothing, gasped once or twice and expired. Olive moved a little and lay down by her side, and saw the Indian in the act of loading his gun, and expected he would shoot her next. Full of the dreadful thought, she says, "I hid my face among the leaves and lay waiting the fatal shot. I remained in the same posture till I thought he had taken time enough to kill me, if he intended it, and then raised my head, very cautiously, as you may well suppose, and just caught a glimpse of his back, running from us. It was a happy relief; for although I was not agitated, yet there was a kind of uneasy suspense, and a degree of dread, of I know not what, upon my mind. I soon arose and sat up. It was still; not a breath of air to stir the leaf of a bush; the silence of death was around us. My brother and sister sat up. We were a desolate little company. I looked first at my mother, lying dead at my side, next at them, and then thought to myself, what shall we do? What course shall we take? I was neither terrified nor disheartened, but full of hope that we should be able to get back again to our old place. I told them we would go down the river. I knew we came up the stream, and was sensible we must follow it down, in order to return home.— My sister did not want to go. She was troubled. What shall we do with mother? We cannot do any thing with her, I said, and it can do no good to stay by her. She seemed afraid. The Indians will catch us, and what will become of us? I replied, they can do no more than kill us, and we shall die any how, if we stay here. She hesitated, and still seemed at a loss, and I went on and pointed out to her what we could do. I told her we could find our way along a little Indian path, part of the distance, and then we could turn off and go to the river and make that our guide. Think of the situation we were in. My mother lay dead upon the ground; the babe was carried off we knew not whither; and we three little motherless children, without a mouthful of food, had a lonely, dismal road of fifty or sixty miles, through the wilderness, to travel, before we could reach the habitations of our friends.— However, I did not think much about distances, or difficulties. One thought filled my mind, and that was to get back to the spot from whence we were taken. And I felt not at all discouraged but got up and took my brother Stephen on my back, and spoke to my sister to run along in the path before me, which she readily did. We started and went forward a few yards, and appeared to be getting along well enough, when suddenly a voice rung in our ears. Somebody shouted after us. It was sorrowful hearing. There, said my sister, I told you the

Indians would be after us and catch us again.—
Once more we heard a man crying out to us, and
trying to hail us. I listened and knew his voice.
He spoke with all his might and said, "run, you
dear souls, run." I leaped for joy with the boy upon my back. Oh, how light of heart and happy
we felt, when we found our friends so hear. We
flew to meet them. The sun was not yet down,
and our people did not seem to know whether their
lurking and terrible foes had entirely left the ground
or not. They were eager to make enquiries about
the Indians. They wanted to know if any of them
were killed. I told them there were some; I saw
one shot down with my own eyes. They felt for
us, and were willing to feed us, but all the bread
they had was but two biscuit, one of which they
broke and divided among us children. This bit
of biscuit, you may be assured, was a sweet mor-
sal to our hungry appetites. You might suppose
that now our kind friends and neighbors, who had
taken us under their protection, would be in haste
to leave the ground and advance toward the river,
in pursuit of an apparently defeated and flying foe.
But no, they understood too well the nature of Indian warfare to lay aside their caution and rush
heedlessly on. They might get into a trap before
they were aware of it. They therefore did not
quit their stations, but kept watching at their trees
till after sunset. They then ventured down to
where the Indians had lain, and found their packs
upon the ground which, in their haste to get away,
they had left behind them. There they saw my

poor, dear mother, stretched upon the cold earth, a bloody, murdered corpse. Her they were compelled to leave, but her children, who were painted after the Indian fashion, they took and carried down the hill and left them at the point of a ledge, near the river. With us they left Oliver Bennet, one of their party, whose arm had been broken by a bullet, just below the elbow. They then started off again in pursuit of their scattered enemies. Before they went, Swift, the leader of the party, told the wounded man that when they were on their return they would whistle, and he must answer, and that he and his little company must, on no account, leave their post till after dark, lest the Indians should get upon their track and follow them. We obeyed orders and kept our place, lying near each other, and whispering together. At length I heard a whistle. Bennet thought it might be the Indians. I knew better, I was sure it was our people. Once more the shrill whistle rung through the forest. It stirred my soul, and I whistled back again. Then they came right to us. Our friends, having found the tomahawks of the Indians along with their packs, went immediately to cutting dry poles to make a raft, on which to float down the river.— They soon accomplished their object, got upon their little frail bark, taking us kindly with them, and dropped silently down the stream. It was the last act of a day which, to us motherless and destitute children, had been trying and eventful in no common degree. On this single day we had been in the midst of noise, confusion and death; had seen

our dear mother fall;, were left without food in a
wilderness, at a distance from the white settlements,
and yet at the close of it, found ourselves in the
midst of warm friends, and on our way homeward.
It was a bright moonlight night, and the frost glist-
ened upon the trees, as we floated quietly along,—
At the dawn of the day we came to Wylusing isl-
and. It was now just a week since we were taken
prisoners; and what a week it had been to us, you
can easily imagine. The events of it, and many
of the words which were spoken, are even now, at
my advanced age, more fresh in my mind than the
occurrencies of the past week. We lay by a
whole day at this place, not daring to go forward,
lest we should be discovered by our enemies, who
might, for aught we knew to the contrary, be lurking near the shore, and could single us out and
shoot us at their leisure, without at all exposing
themselves. We had still sixty miles to go, by the
course of the river, before we could reach the habitations of our friends, and we were nearly in a
state of starvation. One biscuit only remained,
and our kind neighbors, who had hazarded their
lives for our rescue, were really afraid that the
younger children would die for want of food. But
the good providence of him who led Israel through
the desert was over us. On Sabbath morning
some one of the party shot a duck, and before night,
a wild turkey. The same day they found an old
canoe at the island, and said they would send the
wounded man and the children down the river in
that. They took it and cleared the sand and stuff

out of it, and we set sail again, at evening, upon our miserable water craft, consisting of the pole raft and the old leaky canoe. They spread a blanket on the bottom for the children to lie on, I was next to the wounded man in the fore part, and a man sat at the hinder end to paddle. As the old canoe leaked, we had plenty of water, and that cold enough too, to lie in. However, we bore it bravely for we felt too intent on escaping and getting home, to mind much about a little discomfort to the body; though if we had been in easy and pleasant circumstances, we might have felt it rather hard to be wet with cold water all night. In the morning one of the party was sent on with the wounded man, and we were taken on board the raft, where we continued till we arrived at Wilksbarre, which was on Wednesday, The people, some how or other, had got wind of our coming, and many of them were out along the banks of the river waiting for us, anxious to know who had returned, and how we were, and what was the news about the Indians. They had sent for our father, that he might be there to meet his family as soon as they should arrive. He came : we saw him ; but, poor man, he looked as though he had passed through a fit of sickness.— Desolate he was indeed. His house was burned, and his wife and children were gone, and he had great reason to fear that he should never see or hear from them again. It was a great relief from his state of suspense and anxiety to see them once more, and to learn something certain about their fate.— Still the loss of his faithful partner, who had struggled with him through so many difficulties, was distressing and sorrowful, and it grieved him much to have to part with his dear little child, torn away from his fond embraces, and probably murdered by the enemy. There was, notwithstanding, some sad comfort in the thought that they had passed away beyond the reach of their foes into the silent chambers of death, where, in the beautiful language of Job, "the wicked cease from troubling and the weary are at rest, the prisoners rest together, they hear not the voice of the oppressor."

Mr. Franklin and his children went directly back to Nanticoke and lived near the spot where the house stood which the Indians had burned. Having returned to the old place, and into the midst of objects familiar to her, Mrs. Stevens found inducements and leisure for reflection. Often, she remarks, in the course of the summer following, was I overcome with my feelings in thinking over what we had gone through, and about the death of my dear mother, and the loss of the little child. I could see and feel the loss of both, much more sensibly, than at the time when it first took place. Then there was such a stir and excitement in me, and about me, that I could scarcely tell whether I felt her death at all. I knew it as though I knew it not; I had no time to reflect upon it. But afterwards, when the struggle and excitement of the trying time had passed away, the tide of thought and feeling returned upon me, and I wept for those whose faces I was never again to behold in this world,

CHAPTER V.

Abortive attempt of Mr. Franklin to settle at Chokenet, up the Susquehannah river—Hindered by the early and severe cold of the winter of 1784—Sufferings of Arnold Franklin and two other men up the Susquehannah during the winter of 1784 and 1785—Description of the ice freshet in the spring of 1783 or 4.

We have seen the family settled quietly again at their old home, but their changes and troubles were not ended. The war between the settlers in the valley of Wyoming, and the British and Indians had abated, only to be followed by a revival of the the old quarrel between them and the Pennamites; and Mr. Franklin, worn out with these everlasting contentions about the title of the land, determined to leave it. The place he chose was called Chokenet, up the Susquehannah river 140 miles above Wilksbarre, and not far from Chenango point. To make provisions for a removal, he went up in the summer, and cut and secured a quantity of hay. This was soon after the war. The calculation was to go up the river in the fall with a boat, and to carry provisions and other necessary matters sufficient to last through the winter, expecting to move the family in the spring; but cold weather set in so early and so severely that this part of the plan had to be given up.

Arnold Franklin, his adopted son, and two other men went by land, carrying a small quantity of provisions and some cooking utensils, having each of them a horse, and each driving a yoke of oxen. Mr. Franklin himself went with them, a part or all the way, but returned immediately to bring on, in a boat, such food as would be necessary to sustain them during the winter. The early shutting up of the river by frost, prevented him from doing it, and there came on such early and deep snows, that there was no such thing as his going back to them, or their returning to him. It was almost an unbroken wilderness, and there could not be said to be any proper road through it. It was a dismal prospect to the three poor fellows, shut up there in the woods, so far from any inhabitants, with only a few weeks provisions, and with no prospect of any relief from abroad, through all the stormy months of a long dreary winter. The winters of this period are famous in our American annals, for the intense severity of its cold, and the depth of its snows. The fact may be well remembered by many now living. In this cheerless situation they had some relief from the prospect of absolute starvation.—They could kill an ox and subsist on the beef until the spring opened upon them. This was encouraging, and they comforted themselves with the thought. Judge then their feelings when, upon going abroad one morning, they found that their three yoke of oxen, upon which they depended so much, had all fallen through the ice and floated down the river entirely beyond their reach. Their hopes of living through the winter began now to grow dim, though they did not lie down in dispair. Having a small quantity of corn meal on hand, they put themselves upon an allowance of one spoonful each per day. The meal was soon expended. They then concluded to kill one of their horses, and drew lots which it should be, and the lot fell on the least valuable of the three. They killed it and subsistsd upon its flesh until spring, when the river opened and their hopes revived.— They immediately shipped the few effects they had on board a canoe, and started for home, expecting to go by water all the way. Their only provision was the hide of the old horse. which they roasted well before they set out, and which was their breakfast, dinner and supper every day. Probably it relished as well to their keen appetites, and hungry stomachs, as the best beef-stake does to the full fed epicure. They hoped, when they set out, that they should find an open river and fair sailing all the way; judge then their surprise and consternation to find, before they had proceeded far, the river completely blocked up with ice, leaving no possibility of proceeding further by water. Their hopes died within them. The snow was so deep they could not travel by land; they were shut out from the water; what should they do? Should they sink down in despair and die, or make an effort to see what could be done? Life is dear, and not to be yielded without a struggle. They searched and made a trial, and found that the ice would support them. So they hauled up their canoe, packed up their things and started on foot. Pinched by famine, with death staring them in the face, exhausted and dispirited in no slight degree, their case was desperate. They did not, however, quite give up, but persevered and proceeded on their way, "faint yet pursuing." But, poor fellows, new troubles awaited them, they found the river open again, their comfortable turnpike of ice was wholly taken away, and they had no longer any such thing as a solid road to bear up their weary footsteps. They then thought they would make the attempt to go by land, notwithstanding the depth of snow. Soon after, they found a small Indian canoe, and with much effort, in their weak condition, dragged it into the water. They found upon trial that it would not bear them up, except as two of them lay down, while one sat up and steered. In this ill provided and unpromising state, they floated down the river and arrived safely at their home, having barely escaped, to use the expressive language of Job, " with the skin of their teeth." The removal of Mr. Franklin's family to Chokenet was defeated. His team had been drowned, and the ice freshet which took place this spring, swept away his provisions, and he found himself unprepared for so distant an expedition. He, however, with three other families, commenced a settlement, a year or two after, at a place called Wysox, about 60 miles up the river.

I proceed now to give some account of the ice freshet which took place, as is supposed, in the spring of 1783 or 4.

The ice froze this winter to an uncommon thickness. About the first of March a severe thaw attended with rain began; and from the depth of the ice, and the suddenness of the thaw, people, who lived along the banks of the river, expected, when it should break up, that it would make terrible work every where within the sweep of the stream. Their dismal forebodings soon began to be realized. Not far from the first of March, toward evening, the water began to pour over the ice, along the channel of the river, and also to run round next to the foot of the hills where the land was a little lower than near the banks, thus forming an island round the houses of the settlers, which stood on the highest part of the flats. Just at evening the whole body of ice broke and started down stream in one wild and terrific mass, which threatened to carry every thing before it. The men belonging to the settlement were out upon the watch, seeking to evade, if possible, a conflict with the mighty foe which they saw bearing down upon them. Mr. Franklin was the owner of a boat, which he had run into a cove out of the current, and laid up for winter; and he and others went in haste to clear out the ice and get it ready. in case it should be wanted. While they were out upon this business, they found that the ice had lodged below, in a narrow place between the hills, and had formed a dam across the stream, which checked the impetuosity of the current, and caused the water to set back like a pond. He left the men at their work, with directions to bring the boat on as soon as possible, and hastened back to take care of his family. When he reached the house he found the children in bed, got them up immediately, and proceeded to a large two story block house, which had been built and used as a fort in time of the war. This building stood on ground a little raised above the general surface of the flats, and was the only shelter within reach which promised any thing like safety during the night. As they were pressing forward, Mrs. Franklin recollected that they had brought no provisions, and observed to her husband that the children would want something to eat. He left them to go on by themselves, and returned and procured some bread, and although he made good speed, the water was nearly up to his waist before he arrived at the block house. Previous to this six other families had got in. He had scarcely entered when the water followed, rushing into the house with a great noise, and pouring into the cellar at the same time, it threatened to flood them in their place of refuge, and constrained them to climb up into the chamber. This they did with much difficulty and confusion, by means of a ladder. They were all in the dark, fire put out, the women and children weeping, crying and screaming within, all in a hurry to get up the ladder at once, haunted by fears of drowning, mothers fearing for their children, children crying out to their mothers; altogether it was a scene of confusion which no tongue or pen of mortal can adequately describe. They succeeded finally in getting into the upper story without the loss of life or limb. Not very long after this the men whom

Mr. Franklin had left in charge of his boat came on with it. The water continued to rise till it reached the second story, and the men brought the boat up to the windows, on the lower side, out of the way of the large masses of ice which kept constantly coming and jarring against the logs of the fort as if they meant to break it down. While the boat lay thus against the leward side of the building, some young women ventured into it, through a window, attracted probably by the fire which they saw in the boat, which the men on board had kept burning during the night. The calculation was to have the boat ready, so that if the house went, all its inmates might get into it and be rowed or pushed ashore. The boat was large enough for this purpose, being of the description then called Middletown boats, and capable of carrying nine or ten tons. There was great reason to fear that they would be constrained to attempt an escape before the dawn of day. They could hear the cakes of ice dash and jamb against the logs of the old fort, and feel it tremble and shake as if in an ague fit; and this not once or twice, but jamb, jamb, shake, shake, roar, roar, all the time, every moment.— Whilst they were in this state of agitation, looking out for breakers continually, they saw, to their terror and amazement, late in the night, an immense mass of ice moving majestically down the stream right in the direction of the house. They expected it would strike the building, and knew if it did it would carry it away. It was a fearful sight to see it towering above the floods, and advancing with a force which no human power could stay for a single moment. In silent and blank amazement they stood and waited the dreadful onset. It regarded not the feelings of the tremblers within the fort, but marched steadily up as if to take the place by storm, when suddenly it was arrested. It stopped so near the walls that, when the water dried away, they found only room enough for a man to pass through. Instead of being a destroyer it proved a safeguard. It was several rods in length, much longer than the fort, extending out beyond it on either hand. It was also as high as the walls, and was bedded firmly in the soil, and thus was able to resist, and did actually resist, and ward off all attacks of the ice, which still continued to sweep around it. The cause of its grounding was its great weight, it being composed of cakes of ice heaped one upon another; and this was occasioned by the setting back of the water from the dam below, and by the constant accumulation of ice from above, by the strong current of the river. Probably also there were special objects which helped to increase the size of this mountain of ice. It grounded in ten feet of water, and produced at once a very observable and very welcome change, both out of the house and within it. The tumult of the waves and the noise of the dashing pieces of ice were no longer heard, and the cries of the children were hushed. Oh, it was a happy escape, and a joyful moment. The goodness of God was visible in it.— At length, this long and dismal night, which appeared like an age to those who were confined within the chamber of the fort, came to a close, and the welcome light of the morning dawned upon them. They could look abroad now and see some of the effects of the flood. On the opposite side of the river a number of houses which had been swept from their foundations, and completely merged under the water and ice, except a part of the roof, were visible, and the families which dwelt in them had crawled up and were seated upon the ridge.— Mr. Franklin's house was swept away with all its contents; all his domestic animals were drowned; not so much as a fowl was left. Add to this the entire destruction of his winter grain, of which he had twenty or thirty acres sown upon the flats, and consider this a specimen of what befel several other families, and you will have a faint picture of the desolation caused by the raging of the elements.

Let us return to the fort. By the light of day its imprisoned inmates could see how to effect their escape. The water was still up, ten feet deep in places, but it was calm, though covered with fragments and cakes of ice, and they got out of the upper story, and by means of boards, which they laid from one large cake of ice to another, they all reached the shore in safety. One young woman fell in, by setting her foot upon a place which was not solid, and the small pieces of ice closed over her, and she would have been drowned but for her long head of hair, which floated upon the surface. A man saw it, caught hold of it, and drew her out.

Mr. Franklin's crop, as I stated above, was destroyed, and instead of a harvest of grain, such as he had once expected, he found a harvest of ice.— It was heaped up in such immense masses that some portion of it remained till August. No grain could grow that season on that part of his flats. There was so much ice covered up and preserved, as in an ice house, that people procured it, as late as August, to make ice punch. Thus ended this scene of imminent danger, and providential deliverance.

CHAPTER VI.

Settlement of the family at Wysox—Removal thence to the Lake country—Difficulties encountered by the way, and after their arrival —Death of Mr. Franklin—Conclusion.

This spring the family moved up the river to Wysox, being destitute, almost entirely, of provisions and clothing. By great exertions a little wheat had been saved from the desolating flood, but all their clothes, except those they wore upon their backs, were carried down the river. This was immediately after the distresses of the Revolutionary war, and thus, troubles after troubles, rolled their relentless waves over them. Yet they were neither forsaken nor discouraged. The Lord preserved them. He had given them resolute hearts and active hands, and Mr. Franklin and his wife and children, as soon as they were settled in their new place of residence, set themselves at work with great diligence. They plowed and planted, and a beautiful corn harvest rewarded their toil that summer, and by dint of hard labor they soon began to thrive again. They resided at Wysox five years. Somewhere within that period, probably near the middle, another freshet was experienced, familiarly known as the "Pumpion Fresh." This flood was in the fall, when the river flats were covered with ripe corn, much of it ungathered, and loaded with an extraordinary quantity of pumpions, which floated down the stream in such numbers as almost to cover its entire surface; and hence the name of the freshet. Mr. Franklin had wheat stacked, which was very near being swept away. All the stacks floated, but by great effort a little was saved for the use of the family. As to the harvest of Indian corn, the bulk of it was gathered, but not till after it had been buried in sand and gravel, so long and in such a wet state, as nearly to destroy it. Much the larger portion was fit only for hogs, and not good for them, being partly rotten and mouldy, and gritty.

After the expiration of five years, spent at this place, Mr. Franklin, having previously explored and prepared the way in some measure, set out with his family for the "Lake Country," in the state of New-York. They began their laborious journey in the month of March, in sleighs. They had hills, and even mountains to climb and to cross, rendered dangerous and almost impassable by precipices, ice, rocks and trees. Some part of the way they had to wade through torrents of water, holding on upon the sleighs to keep them from floating down stream. They struggled on their journey in water, out of water, sometimes swamped in mud, and sometimes tugging through snow. In one instance they traversed a mountain, between Wysox and Newtown, (Elmira) where no team had ever been before, and where they had to cut their way through the forest by the most unsparing labor, and with the most unflinching resolution. They reached Newtown after many laborious days of travel. Thence their route was to the head of the Seneca Lake, down the lake and through the outlet, in boats, into the Cayuga; thence up the lake to where the village of Aurora now stands. They encamped some days near the head of the Seneca, on account of the prevalence of strong north-west winds. They found here an opportunity to unload and rest themselves awhile, after the excessive fatigues and privations they had undergone.

Having recruited a little, and the wind proving favorable, they floated down the deep blue waters of the Seneca, with light and buoyant hearts, and high hopes of a speedy termination of their voyage. But their difficulties were not yet at an end. They found the falls and rapids of the Seneca river very troublesome, and were in great danger of unshipping all their cargo. They had to stop and unload a part, and carry over the remainder and leave it, and then return for the half left behind.— Such were the dangers and delays of this part of the passage that the boats carried no persons except those who managed them. Before the families arrived at the foot of the falls the boat went down, and by the time the family came the boat was unloaded; the men started with the boat for the head of the falls, part of the time wading in the cold water and drawing the boat against a heavy and powerful stream, to get the remainder of the load, which contained about all their clothes, beds and provisions. But night came on and they could not descend in the dark, and they had to remain till the morning. Meantime the families having seen the dangers of the falls, and seeing no return of the men, they very naturally supposed the current had dashed them among the rocks and all was destroyed. The families, consisting of women and children, and one of the young women having but a few days before been married to one of the men who had gone up the falls, now felt themselves as destined to the most distressing and certain ruin. Hope seemed to flee, and the most heartrending anguish preyed upon them. They wandered up and down the stream with painful anxiety till the snow came so fast they huddled up, as it were, in a little pile, over a spark of fire which remained, weeping and wringing their hands with anguish, till morning, when to the great joy of all, the boat returned safe and took the ltitle weary company on board. They had no further impediments till they reached the Cayuga, but here they were stopped. They found the lake full of ice, and had to cut a passage through it for their boat. It took them several days to get only six miles, and they had to work smartly for this. This was another disappointment, for they had previously expected to reach the point of their destination in a single day, and might easily have done it if there had been no obstruction. One morning, however, after this, they awoke, and to their great joy, found the ice all gone. It all went in one night. Not a particle of it remained to show that there had ever been such an article there. Its disappearance was probably owing to the operation of the south wind. The particular process is left for the consideration of philosophers. Having now a clear sea, their voyage was soon concluded.— They landed near the spot now occupied by the village of Aurora. Here they were, a little secluded band of settlers. Not a human soul, Indian or white, was living there at the time. The Indians all went off in the time of Sullivan's campaign, or soon after, and did not return till after the Franklin family had settled at the place. This summer (1789) was a time of extraordinary scarcity. Many families, in the back parts of N. York and Pennsylvania, lived mostly on greens, for a considerable time before harvest. Mr. Franklin had stored a quantity of grain near Tioga Point, and had also deposited a barrel of pork and a barrel of flour there, which Roswell and his brother-inlaw went for but did not find. It had been eaten up, or disposed of. The grain was burnt with the mill in which it had been stored. Finding no flour, pork nor grain at Tioga Point, the two young men proceeded on down the Susquehannah to Wysox, where a small quantity of rye was left behind, when the family removed. This they thrashed, had ground, and brought home to Cayuga. They were absent five weeks, during which time the family was destitute of bread. They subsisted on the milk of their cows chiefly, with the rare addition, sometimes, of a few ground nuts, which they roasted, and found very palatable and wholesome.

Besides the inconvenience of being pinched for bread, they had to pass the summer in a little cramped bit of a shantee. However, in the fall, they were able to erect a comfortable log house, in which they wintered as happily, perhaps, as they would have done in an elegant brick house. There was now, after so many changes and privations, a fair prospect of a permanent and undisturbed settlement for Mr. Franklin and family. The coast was clear, and the land was good. Every thing which they put in the ground grew and prospered wonderfully. As soon as they were able to plough and sow, and reap, they found themselves in one of the finest wheat countries in the world. Where the land was well prepared, and seasonably sowed, it produced from twenty or thirty, to forty, or, in some rare instances, fifty bushels to the acre.— All other kinds of grain did admirably well. The earth brought forth in abundance. Their situation began to be prosperous and flattering. Hope danced before them and beckoned them forward to future years of earthly abundance and comfort. But such prospects are not to be relied on. They had no title to their land, and this exposed them to a loss. When they went on they expected to buy or lease from the Indians, in whose hands it then was.

But in this they were defeated. For, not far from this time, the government of the state held a talk with the Indians, and concluded a treaty, under which a large tract of land was purchased, afterwards known by the name of the military tract.— It bore this name because it was granted to the troops for military services performed during the war of the Revolution. Hence a lease from the Indians was of no account. Another trouble was that Mr. Franklin had, without knowing it, built upon that portion of the land which the Indians had reserved for themselves. This was not owing to any want of care on his part, for he had been at the pains of making particular enquiries, as far as he had opportunity, and supposed himself entirely clear from any danger of interfering with the rights of the natives. But when the state surveyors came on and laid out the lots, according to treaty, his house and half his improvements fell within the Indian line. Moreover, so many others had planted themselves on their reservation, that the Indians complained to the Governor, (George Clinton) who thereupon issued a proclamation, warning the people to leave the reserved lands, and forbidding any one, thereafter, to settle upon them. The intruders paid no attention to the proclamation, and the Indians continued to complain, till the Governor sent on a sheriff and posse of fifty men to dispossess them. They did it thoroughly; turned thirteen or fourteen families adrift, and burnt their houses. Mr. Franklin's was near the line, and he petitioned the sheriff to let him remain till spring. His request was granted provided he could satisfy the Indians. Before the time came when he was to leave his house, he agreed with a man, who had recently come into the settlement, to procure a title to that part of the lot not within the forbidden bounds, on which his improvement lay. An agreement was entered into between them, and this man was to have one half of the land for his pains. He was plausible enough in making the bargain, and wore a fair face before Mr. Franklin, and probably did not, at the time, deliberately intend to pursue the vile course which he afterwards took. However this might have been, he actually most basely betrayed the trust reposed in him. He went below, found the owner, got a friend to join him, and they two bought the lot, (640 acres) out from under Mr. Franklin, at a low price, not more than fifty cents per acre, and then had the villainous hardihood to return and dispossess him, and would not allow him any share in his own improvements. This was such a base piece of treachery, on the part of one whom Mr. Franklin had regarded and treated as a friend, that it entered like a knife into his soul, and wounded him deeply. He was, at the same time, in a broken and miserable state of health, and being unable to obtain relief from government, or from any other quarter, he fell into deep melancholy, which brought on a despairing, forsaken frame of feeling, as though every thing was, and must be fatally against him, and as though no creature or thing on earth could ever smile on him more. For several weeks he went about in this forlorn and utterly comfortless state of mind, avoiding company and conversation almost all the time, appearing solitary in the midst of his family, no longer taking any interest in their concerns, as he had formerly done. The family felt anxious about him, and watched him, having fears that he might be overcome and get bewildered, and be led to aim a fatal blow at his own life.

In addition to what was stated above concerning the manner in which the man who wronged him was treated by Mr. Franklin, it may here be observed, that he supplied him, in his poverty, (for he was a broken merchant and brought little into the country but that horrid commodity, a barrel of rum) with a team and farming tools, and gave him liberty to plough and sow, within his enclosure, and put into the ground all he could, and did not charge him a cent. And when he brought on his family, the next spring, Mr. Franklin took them into his house, and suffered them to live there all summer without demanding pay for his trouble, and placed so much confidence in him, that the agreement entered into betweem them was not committed to writing. The conduct of this person, on this occasion, is one proof, among ten thousand, of the truth of the scripture declaration, that "the love of money is the root of all evil" The prospect of gain induced him to commit an act of gross injustice, aggravated by vile ingratitude, and consummated by brazen impudence. It would have softened his crime, in some degree, and would have caused his conduct to sit less sorely upon Mr. Franklin if he would have allowed him to retain a part of his improvements. But no, he had the power in his hands, and he determined to hold on upon the whole possession. After this, perhaps two or three weeks after the return of this man from the east, Mr. Franklin, whose melancholy did not abate, was observed to be absent from the house longer than usual, on a certain day. The family began to be concerned about him. Mrs. Franklin went to Roswell, who was at work near the house, and requested him to go and see what had become of his father. He left his work immediately, and followed a foot path which led along down the lake shore, the only road travelled at that time. When he had pursued this track sixty or seventy rods, he discovered a rope lying on one side of it. He looked at it, and knew that he had seen it that morning in the stable. This alarmed him. He continued to search round about through the grove, and on his return, within about forty rods of the house, found him lying on the ground, dead. He had shot himself, and had made his arrangements to do it, with that exactness and care not to be defeated, which melancholy and tempted persons usually evince. It appeared, by what they could discover, that he had cocked his gun, fixed the breech in an old stump, whittled a stick, with a crotch at one end, to push against the trigger, had put the muzzle into his ear, and then, by means of his stick, had fired it off. The muzzle being held close within the ear, made no appearance of a hurt on the side where the charge went in, but where it came out it tore his head and made a frightful wound. The family had heard the gun, but it was common for Indians and others to shoot in the woods, and the report did not occasion any uneasiness at first. It was his long absence, and not the sound of the gun which awakened their fears.— Roswell, having looked upon the sad corpse of his poor melancholy father, turned mournfully away, and moved slowly toward the house. Mrs. Franklin was on the watch, and as he drew near, saw that something of a distressing nature had happened, for he looked as pale as a cloth, and seemed as one struck dumb with amazement. " What is the matter? What has become of him? Is he dead?" Roswell made no answer at first. How could he? In what language could he break the dreadful news? She went to him and repeated her enquiries; and, at length, he told her his father was no more. The shock was overpowering. So sudden a departure into the world of spirits, of a husband and father, would, at any time, or under any circumstances, have been affecting. But to fall as he did shrouded in gloom, assailed by temptation, and driven to despair; to fall by his own hand, as one to whom life, so dear to us all, had become an intolerable burden. This was indeed a heavy stroke to the family, the heaviest of all which had hitherto befallen them. They had gone through great privations and hardships, had often been reduced very low, but had risen again, and while the father and head of the family lived, had a leader,

and could cheer one another with the prospect of
better times. Now they are desolate; they are
dumb with grief. But the pressure of want would
not suffer them to sit still and brood over their
troubles and sink down into despair. If they had
had wealth and leisure, they might have done it.
Poverty was a blessing to them. They must work
or starve. They had been trained up in habits of
industry, and they were willing to put their shoulders to the wheel and lift. Though sorrowful, they
were not discouraged. God did not forsake them
in the time of their affliction, and their heavy losses. They had been accustomed to the loss of property, and they had always risen again by persevering industry. That is the way to rise, and God
will bless their efforts. If people must lose their
living, which perhaps they have earned by stren-
uous efforts, let them not lose their courage, let them
not think their lot hard; that reflects upon God.—
Let them set themselves at any business which
comes to hand; let them trust the Lord and go a-
head, and a way will be opened for them It is
good to be humbled, but never best to be discouraged.

The death of Mr. Franklin was in 1791, or 2,
as near as is remembered. Mrs. Franklin was
strong and healthy, and of good courage, and able
to do the work within doors. The out-door work
was performed by the sons, Roswell and Stephen.
Roswell, the eldest son, was strong, accustomed to
hardships, and able to endure them. Stephen, who
was several years younger, had been crippled in

his arms, when a child, by the small pox, and could not perform the heaviest kind of work; and even if he had been sound, he was but a boy when his father died. The main burden fell, of course, upon the eldest, who was twenty one when they first came to the country, and twenty three at the death of his father. He hired of the Indians that part of his father's clearing which lay on the Reservation, paid them a stipulated rent, and by dint of persevering industry, with his own hands, and by the blessing of God, raised sufficient grain for the support of the family.

The family lived in their own house, and worked upon rented land, until after the Indians sold out to the state. After this sale the legislature passed a law to give those settlers, who had been on the ground several years, a right to buy in preference to new comers, at the avarage price of new lands.

This was called the Pre-emption right.

Roswell bought, and has lived there and in the vicinity ever since, and is now (1838) an old man of seventy. It may be interesting to mention that there is not a man now living in the county of Cayuga, who has been in it as long as he, to wit, forty-nine years in April, 1838. There were other young men who came in soon after, of whom some are dead and others still survive.

What wonderful changes Western New-York has seen since that period. Indians, then owners of the soil over which they roamed, chased the deer through their native forests. White men came and crowded them out; and where are they now? They have melted away like the snow before the southern breezes of the spring. The face of the fertile country where they hunted and fished, and raised their scanty crops of maize, is studded with the habitations of white men, as thick as stars. Roads have been opened, canals dug, rail-roads constructed, villages and cities built, as if by miracle; and what was the "Ultima Thule" of the New Englanders, fifty years ago, is now the centre of the world. It is but a step now from Boston to Buffalo, and not so far to the Rocky Mountains as it was then to the Genesee River. The progress of this country in population, wealth and power, is more marvelous than any one of the seven wonders of the world; if not beyond all of them combined. This is no reason why we should glory in man, or even boast of the vigor of our free institutions. There is reason for gratitude to God, and perhaps some ground for rejoicing in the happiness of our lot, but it should be with trembling.

We should remember that men are depraved and blinded creatures, always prone to depart from God, and to run eagerly after those objects which will work their ruin. It ought to be understood that the stability of the country depends upon the favor of God, and that this can be enjoyed only as his laws are obeyed. If men will be greedy of gain; if they will run into luxuries; if they will quaff the intoxicating cup; if they will sell themselves to the selfish schemes of a bigoted party spirit; if they will trample upon the Sabbath, and will not repent and obey the gospel; what can be expected but that the judgments of God will fall and wither the strength of the young giant of the West? Woe be to the land when God forsakes it; and forsake it he will, unless there be such repentance, prayer and effort, as shall stay and turn back the tide of ungodliness.

In this work of reform, every one capable of knowing his duty ought to begin with himself, with his own heart and life. Let us see to it that we do not cherish sin, not even in thought, for if we do, the Lord will not hear our prayers. Let the drunkard put away his cups, the swearer his oaths, the sabbath breaker his violations, and sinners of every description, their evil practices.— Let not those who are outwardly moral imagine they can stand before God. They have sinned, and must repent; they are defiled and must be washed in the great fountain opened by the death of Christ; they are propense to evil and backward to good, and need the holy truths of the bible, applied by the Holy Spirit to the conscience and the heart. In reference to the process required for purifying the land and sustaining the great interests of piety, knowledge, law and liberty; heads of families ought, universally, to take a leading and active part. Let them not plead ignorance, or weakness, to excuse themselves from doing their duty. Do you seek light; if not, how dare you presume to plead your want of it as an excuse? What! you are *too ignorant* are you? And yet you are not seeking to know your duty. How does this look? Will this excuse stand before God? If you find you lack knowledge, why are you not reading, thinking, praying and striving to acquire it? Is it not written in a certain old and true book, "If any man lack wisdom let him ask of God, who giveth to all liberally, and upbraideth not, and it shall be given him." But you are *too weak*. Are you too weak to tell your children that they are sinners, and dying creatures; or to point out to them their faults, and take pains to have them amended? Are you too weak to give them a plain account of a Saviour, of his being born of a woman, of his going about doing good, of his dying love, of his rising from the dead, of his going up into heaven to appear before God, in behalf of all who come to God by him? Are you too weak to hold them back from what you know to be sinful, or to correct them with the rod when you find that good instructions, and kind words, will not produce the desired effect? Parents, and heads of families, do your duty; and do not presume to plead your weakness as an excuse, either for total neglect or partial performance.

Ministers and churches should do their part in the great work of purifying the land, and sustaining the great interests of an enlightened piety, and a sound morality. It belongs to them, by the promised aid of the spirit of God, to exert an influence upon the heart and soul; to throw light into the mind, and wake up its dormant energies to the pursuit and practice of virtue and happiness; not mere animal enjoyment, but such happiness as is consistent with the high destinies of an immotal agent.

Fellow christians! look your duty in the face, and do it faithfully.

Legislators and magistrates ought also to consult and act with wisdom and spirit, for the good of the country. Let them legislate upon sound principles; let them be governed, not by the narrow dictates of a selfish party zeal, but by a sacred regard to truth and righteousness. Let them maintain inviolate the majesty of the law, frown upon mobs, assert freedom of speech, and vindicate the right of every one to print and publish what he pleases; amenable to the laws alone for the abuse of that right.

If the leaders of society, from the head of a single family, up to the head of a nation, would do any thing near what they ought in this matter, a generation might be trained up, under the blessing of God, which would make the hills break forth into singing, and cause the trees of the field to clap their hands. Then the devout wish of the inspired psalmist would be realized—" That our sons may be as plants grown up in their youth; that our daughters may be as corner stones polished after the similitude of a palace; that our garners may be full affording all manner of store; that our sheep may bring forth thousands in our streets; that our oxen may be strong to labor; that there be no breaking in, nor going out; that there be no complaining in our streets. Happy is that people that is in such a case; yea, happy is that people whose God is the Lord."

In bringing about this blessed result, the teachers of youth, both male and female, whether employed in common schools, or in the higher seminaries, may exert a most important influence.—They may and ought to do much to train the young for future usefulness in the world; they may contribute even to their eternal salvation, if they pray in faith, and live and act for God. Great is the responsibility which lies upon the present generation; happy will be the results of acting according to it, and deplorable the consequences of disregarding it. We want humility; we want faith, and love, and wisdom, and energy, and union among christians ; and we need the power of the Holy Ghost to move upon the mighty mass of unconverted mind growing up in the country. O, for a spirit of prevailing prayer, accompanied by faithful efforts to do good, on the part of the great body of professing christians and ministers throughout the whole length and breadth of the land; then might the fair skies of this rising republic never be darkened by the black clouds of vengeance, which will gather and burst here, as they have done elsewhere, in other nations, except humble repentance and thorough reform shall be presented, on an extensive scale before the eye of heaven.—God, in his infinite mercy, grant that this may be the case; and that the generations to come may not be buried under the ruins of broken laws, debauched morals, violated sabbaths, accumulated oppressions and disorganized institutions.

"Alas! misfortunes follow in a train,
And oft in life form one perpetual chain;
Fear buries fear, and ills on ills attend,
Till life and sorrow meet one common end."

CONTENTS.

Chapter 1.

Mr. Franklin enlists as a soldier in the British army—Goes to Canada—Thence to the West Indies—Returns to Connecticut—Marries—Goes to Wyoming—Is put in jail at Easton—Breaks jail and escapes—Brings on his family to Wyoming—Is subsequently engaged in several skirmishes with the Pennamites, and with the Indians.   3

Chapter 2.

Battle of Wyoming—Confidence, and appearance of victory on the part of the Americans—Sudden and fatal turn of the action against them—Efforts of Mr. Franklin to retrieve the disasters of the day—Narrowly escapes being killed—Returns to the fort and witnesses the grief of the women and children.   29

Chapter 3.

Flight of the Franklins down the river—They have the small pox—Their return the next spring to their former residence—Loss of the eldest son by the Indians—Capture and return of the second son and his cousin.   38

CONTENTS.

CHAPTER 4.

The mother and four children taken prisoners by the Indians—Pursued by the whites—A skirmish—Mrs. Franklin killed—The youngest child carried off—The others recovered. 55

CHAPTER 5.

Abortive attempt of Mr. Franklin to settle at Chokenet, up the Susquehannah river—Hindered by the early and severe cold of the winter of 1784—Sufferings of Arnold Franklin and two other men, up the Susquehannah, during the winter of 1784 and 1785—Description of the ice freshet in the spring of 1783 or 4. 75

CHAPTER 6.

Settlement of the family at Wysox—Removal thence to the Lake country—Difficulties encountered—Final settlement—Death of Mr. Franklin—Conclusion. 83

Written by Rev. ROBERT HUBBARD.

Published by STEPHEN FRANKLIN.

Milton Keynes UK
Ingram Content Group UK Ltd.
UKHW030403070224
437385UK00006B/362